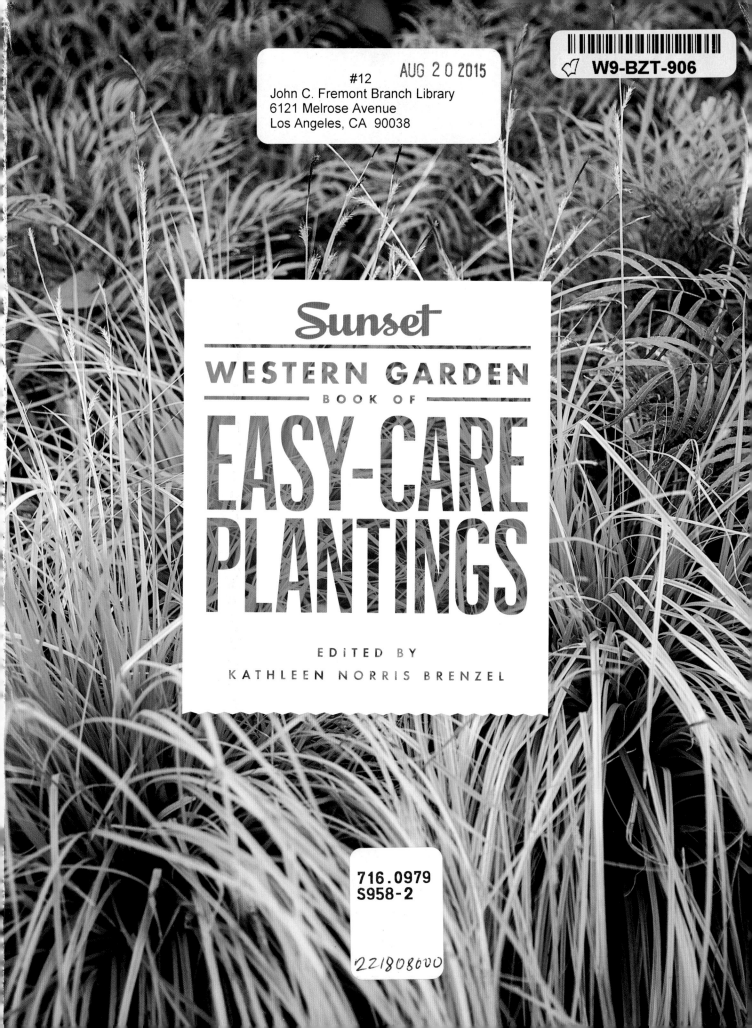

#12
John C. Fremont Branch Library
6121 Melrose Avenue
Los Angeles, CA 90038

AUG 2 0 2015

W9-BZT-906

716.0979
S958-2

221808000

Sunset

WESTERN GARDEN

BOOK OF

EASY-CARE PLANTINGS

EDITED BY

KATHLEEN NORRIS BRENZEL

In Nature's Garden

MARCH 1934   10 CENTS

SUNSET
IN THE BEST HOMES IN THE WEST

FLORAL BOUNTY

▲

ON THE COVER *Sunset* entices readers to head out and see the West's glorious wildflowers—treasures of the moment with a teasing charm—which show up, or not, depending on winter rainfall. Bloom displays such as this continue to inspire gardeners.

◄

IN THE WILD Brittlebush *(Encelia farinosa),* a small perennial shrub with silvery, woolly leaves, unfurls its yellow spring blooms against the craggy basalt cliffs of Superstition Mountain near Apache Junction, Arizona. Widespread throughout the Southwest, brittlebush often grows wild among spiny desert plants such as ocotillo, opuntia, and yucca, and wildflowers such as California poppies, as shown here. In Southwest gardens, give it gritty or sandy soil and little to no irrigation after the first year; it's especially pretty when spilling over sandstone boulders.

Plants make the garden. But we gardeners often choose them for very personal reasons. Maybe a neighbor recommended a hop bush because it grows fast and makes a great screen. Or a gardenia with fragrant white blooms caught your eye at the nursery, or you just need something—anything—to fill that empty patch of dirt out back. "My only plant is a pygmy date palm in a patio pot," says Nino Padova, a *Sunset* travel editor. "But it's a living thing. It makes me feel good to see it thrive. It has changed me, connected me to the natural world." Lauren Dunec Hoang, *Sunset* garden design assistant, attributes her love of gardening to sweet memories of plucking ripe, sun-warmed fruits from her parents' backyard trees on summer afternoons.

My fascination with plants began, not in a garden, but during summertime road trips around the West when I was

CHAPARRAL

▼

GARDEN (below) California lilac (*Ceanothus thyrsiflorus* 'Victoria') pairs well with other unthirsty plants, including the *Rosmarinus officinalis* and *Carex flagellifera* used in this garden. *Ligustrum ovalifolium* 'Aureum' grows behind.

WILD (below, right) *Ceanothus thyrsiflorus* shows off its sky blue spring blooms at Montara Mountain on the San Francisco Peninsula. One of many shrubs making up the dense brush community known as chaparral that cloaks California's coastal hills, it thrives in gritty, fast-draining soil on sun-baked slopes, and can't stand summer water. Natural companions include California fuchsia, woolly blue curls (*Trichostema lanatum*), and blue-flowered *Salvia clevelandii*.

a kid. Ensconced beside three of my siblings in the back seat of my dad's "caddy"—with a fourth up front between Mom and Dad and a family-size tent and a camp stove in the trunk—we'd head out of Santa Monica every summer to some great spot that Dad had no doubt read about in *Sunset* magazine under the headline "the open road is calling." National parks, distant beaches, and deserts—all promised adventure and discovery. Opening the windows, we'd breathe in the sweetly resinous scent of California wild lilacs and scrubland as we traveled the winding roads through the chaparral-covered hillsides outside Los Angeles.

In Sequoia National Park, I marveled at General Sherman, a giant sequoia and one of the largest trees in the world, whose top soared into the clouds. And in Indian Canyons near Palm Springs, the tropical-looking palms mystified me, because I couldn't see the springs that sustained them, beneath a covering of desert sand.

Hiking the trails and scrambling over boulders to take in some of the West's great views, I began to notice and appreciate things. Like how a plant might grow in one spot and nowhere else. The way baby saguaros get their best shot at life in the desert's unforgiving heat by putting down roots in the shade of a mesquite or palo verde "nurse" tree. How redwood forests continually refresh their habitats—old trees fall, decay, and

FOREST

WILD Western hemlock, bigleaf maples, Douglas firs, and spruce trees make up the forest around Sol Duc Falls in Olympic National Park, Washington. Moisture-loving plants such as mosses, lichens, and ferns crowd together in the lush, shady understory, while seedlings germinate in fallen, decaying trees.

GARDEN With its mossy tree stumps and woodland plants, this garden on Vashon Island, Washington, looks as though it might have been lifted intact from a Northwest rain forest. But owners Pat and Walt Riehl were inspired to plant it after visiting Prince Charles's stumpery at High-grove House, then touring gardens with fern expert Martin Rickard, whom they later hired to help them design their own stumpery. They brought in madrone and Douglas fir stumps from construction sites on the island, which Rickard placed among existing trees such as alders, then added ferns and understory woodland plants such as *Epimedium* and *Tolmiea menziesii*. Here, spotted may apple *(Podophyllum* 'Spotty Dotty') fans out its leaves in front of various ferns; tree ferns *(Dicksonia antarctica)* grow behind.
DESIGN Martin Rickard

OAK COUNTRY

▶

WILD Crowned with new green leaves, California valley oaks (*Quercus lobata*) glow in the late afternoon sunlight. By summer, the fresh spring grass around them will have turned golden. Like established oaks throughout California, these venerable trees do not like summer water; in fact, it can kill them.

◀

GARDEN A pocket of unthirsty plants fringes the steps leading upslope in a Tiburon, California, garden. Yellow kangaroo paws, deep burgundy New Zealand flax (*Phormium tenax*), lavender, and tufted green California meadow grass (*Carex pansa*), along with deer grass (*Muhlenbergia rigens*) and *Sedum rupestre* 'Angelina', blend nicely into the natural meadow and oak woodland beyond.
DESIGN Gretchen Whittier

crumble, allowing ferns and young saplings to take root in the spongy, newly replenished earth. In Tuolumne Meadows above Yosemite Valley, near Tenaya Lake where we camped, I wondered how those clusters of red paintbrush and blue lupine poking up through the grasses could bloom so beautifully without benefit of the fertilizers or sprinklers that Dad used back home. I fell in love with the West's great natural landscapes.

But it wasn't until much later, in my first home with a grove of tall redwoods in the backyard, that I began to appreciate the

DESERT

▼

WILD (below, right) In Yaqui Meadows in California's Anza-Borrego Desert State Park, a big ocotillo (*Fouquieria splendens*) is at its spring-season best, with tiny green leaves cloaking bony stems and red flowers at the tips. Smaller chollas dance around it, their spines backlit by the sun, while brittlebush adds a splash of sunny yellow daisies. Grasses carpet the ground between them.

GARDEN (below, left) The Southwest look is similar—mounding shrubs, blond grasses, bony cactus, a splash of blooms, and open spaces. But this front yard, in Tucson, blends tamer plants from the nursery, including an orange-flowered lantana, with cholla behind, agaves near the path, and blond grass in back. DESIGN Elizabeth Przygoda

lessons learned in those varied terrains of my childhood. I planted hydrangeas beneath the redwoods, but they were no match for the tree's thirsty roots, which sucked up water faster than a marathon runner at mile 26. They drooped, badly, after a day or two of heat with no water. Then I remembered the Western sword ferns (*Polystichum munitum*) I'd seen growing naturally in redwood forests, flourishing in dry shade, and planted them. They thrived, putting out lush fronds and always looking fresh despite my lax watering. The secret to an easy-care garden, I learned, is this: Plant what grows naturally in your area, if possible, among plants that have evolved with them. Or group ones from similar climates that are adapted to your region and take the same conditions.

Increasingly, Western gardens are reflecting the shapes and shades of the land, as gardeners make use of their property's natural advantages—its distant views, soils, exposure, climate—and suit the garden to its setting. That might mean bringing in tree stumps, then planting ferns and piggyback plant (*Tolmiea menziesii*) among them to mimic a forest habitat in a Pacific Northwest garden, for example, or replacing a lawn with a mini wildflower meadow in California, or repeating the look of a spruce-and-aspen backdrop by selecting the same plants for a Wyoming garden. Every natural habitat in the West, whether desert cactus or oak woodland, suggests design lessons.

MOUNTAIN

◀

WILD Aspen and spruce trees often grow side by side in northern New Mexico, Colorado, and elsewhere in the southern Rocky Mountains. Together, they create a striking show, especially in fall when the leaves of the quaking aspen *(Populus tremuloides)* turn buttery yellow and tremble in breezes against green spruce foliage. Here, a hawk hovers above the beautiful bands of foliage cloaking the Sangre de Cristo Mountains in the Santa Fe National Forest.

◀

GARDEN For a modern twist, the designer of this garden, in Wyoming's Grand Teton country, evenly spaced aspen trees 6 feet apart in a grid pattern along a sandstone entry walk to show off their slender trunks, then underplanted them with Idaho fescue *(Festuca idahoensis)* and edged them with mounding blue oat grass. Blue-green Colorado spruce trees, beyond, show off their conical shapes against native cottonwoods. **DESIGN** Mark Hershberger

11

WILDFLOWERS—
SOUTHERN CALIFORNIA

◄

GARDEN Inspired by the wildflower fields around her childhood home in rural Southern California, the owner of this backyard, near the foothills in Palo Alto, California, removed a lawn and scattered seeds of orange California poppies (beginning to close in the evening light), along with meadowfoam, blue-eyed grass, pink checkerbloom, and more. The planting changes as poppies finish their bloom cycle and other wildflowers take over; all rest for summer. **DESIGN** Marcia Cross

▼

WILD Every spring (especially after rainy winters), California poppies, yellow goldfields, blue lupines, and other wildflowers paint the Mojave Desert's rolling grasslands, creating one of the West's great spectacles, which naturalist John Muir called "a lake of pure sunshine." The ephemeral flowers have just a few weeks to race from seed to full bloom before summer heat burns them out.

So how do you choose the right plants for your garden—even a small city garden—with all the options available? And how can you blend them with others in a way that makes sense, but with spectacular effects? Most important, are they easy to grow, so you don't need to spend endless hours of precious time tending them? You'll find answers in this book.

As nurseries continue to broaden the choices of colorful, durable plants, easy-care shrubs are the garden's star performers. Focus on those, along with tough but pretty perennials, succulents (where hardy), and grasses, let them scramble in amiable disarray, and they'll demand little in the way of water or maintenance.

EASY-CARE PLANTINGS

This book is all about planting the garden you love, but can leave occasionally, knowing that it will grow well even while you're away. On the following pages, you'll find ideas for plant combinations that thrive without fuss in your part of the West; for creating spectacular effects by pairing plants for texture, size, and shape; and for choosing color schemes that flow together seamlessly. Even if you live in the city, you can surround a patio with plants that blend beautifully, or plant showy gardens in containers.

THE MEDITERRANEAN CONNECTION

If you can peer out your window and see scrubland somewhere in the distance, then you probably live in one of the earth's five Mediterranean climate zones. Besides California and the lands around the Mediterranean Sea, these zones include central Chile, two huge wedges of southern Australia, and the Cape region of South Africa. (Traveling through southern France, Sardinia, and Greece, I have often found myself in landscapes that remind me of home, as the scrubby hillsides in these places have the look and feel of California's chaparral.) All these zones lie on seashores; all have dry summers with little to no rain and mild, wet winters during nondrought years.

Gardeners who use plants that are well adapted to this weather pattern—and there's a surprisingly large palette from which to choose for the West's arid regions—will have few warm-season gardening chores. The familiar herbs such as lavender, rosemary, sage, santolina, and thyme are common choices for good reason: They provide sensual pleasure as well as beauty, and they're tough as nails. California natives, including *Ceanothus*, *Fremontodendron*, and sage, are other handsome choices. Also try kangaroo paw (*Anigozanthos*)

WILDFLOWERS— NORTHWEST, SOUTHWEST

▲

ALPINE (top) Pink mountain heather, red paintbrush, purple lupine, and yellow seep-spring arnica fleck this high meadow in Eight Lakes Basin, Mt. Jefferson Wilderness, Oregon, following snowmelt.

DESERT (bottom) The West's wildflowers are richly varied, depending on location. Here, sand verbena and desert sunflowers thrive in dry washes of Anza-Borrego Desert State Park, California, where they bloom in spring before temperatures soar. Southwest gardeners can get the look with garden-friendly *Verbena gooddingii* and yellow-flowered sundrops (*Calylophus*).

MEDITERRANEAN

◄

WILD In its native Canary Islands, pride of Madeira grows on rocky cliffs and high terraces similar to this one on the headlands of California's Big Sur coastline. The evergreen shrub tolerates drought, brisk ocean winds, and fog, yet pumps out dramatic bloom spires in spring.

▶

GARDEN In Half Moon Bay, California, pride of Madeira pairs well with other tough Mediterranean-climate plants, including vibrant orange-tinged *Leucadendron discolor* and chartreuse-flowered *Euphorbia characias wulfenii*. All tolerate drought, but need soil with excellent drainage.

and *Westringia fruticosa* from Australia; Cape plumbago (*P. auriculata*), *Kniphofia*, and lion's tail (*Leonotis leonurus*) from South Africa; or pride of Madeira (*Echium candicans*) and rockrose (*Cistus*) from the Canary Islands.

We Westerners no longer have the luxury of imposing thirsty garden styles from wetter climates onto our dry land, as populations outgrow water supplies. But if you've grown up in the West, as I have, with hikes in the hills and summer campouts, your garden can be an extension of those adventures—your own bit of wilderness, whether prairie, desert, valley, or forest.

KATHLEEN N. BRENZEL, *SUNSET* **GARDEN EDITOR**

CHAPTER

1

Gardens

Gardeners lucky enough to live on the edge of wild land have a unique opportunity to "borrow" the backdrop and to echo the plantings that grow naturally beyond the garden's boundaries. But even if you live in the heart of San Francisco, or in the suburbs of Seattle or Denver, you can create a garden that looks as if it belongs in your part of the West. The secret: Start with the right plants, whether they're native to your region or simply well adapted to your climate, your garden's exposure (sun or shade, windy or still), and your soil. In arid climates, especially, choose plants that can get by on little water once established.

RIVER VIEW

VANCOUVER, WA When a property has a splendid view, as does this blufftop location overlooking an island in the middle of Lake Vancouver, the temptation might be to clear any vegetation standing in the way. But nothing frames a view like the strong verticals of tree trunks. So the designer added a Japanese maple (*Acer palmatum*) to the left of the path to complement the existing Douglas fir and big-leafed maples (*A. macrophyllum*). The rest of the vegetation was kept extremely simple—just one meadow grass, which mirrors the distant green island. A Carex was originally selected for this space but has been replaced by *Molinia caerulea*, a perennial grass that can take wet winters and heavy frosts. **DESIGN** Karen Ford

DESERT EDGE

◄

SCOTTSDALE, AZ The native desert is just beyond this garden, but it wasn't always accessible. An unbroken stretch of wall separated the wild and cultivated areas, and a large ironwood tree hid the view of the giant saguaro. With the ironwood relocated, a new, segmented wall to frame the majestic saguaro, and steps that invite homeowners and guests into the desert to explore, the boundaries have been blurred. Most of the plants near the garden's walls duplicate those growing in the wild beyond the wall, including several colonies of young saguaros, yellow-flowered brittlebush *(Encelia farinosa)*, and staghorn cholla *(Opuntia versicolor)*. The non-native golden barrel cactus *(Echinocactus gruso-nii)* in the foreground perfectly complements the corrugated texture of the saguaros.
DESIGN Steve Martino

BACKYARD
RETREATS

In a hyper-connected world, your garden is among the few places where you can tune out, find tranquility, and reconnect with nature. No matter how small your space, chances are you can still find a corner of a side yard or backyard for a table and chairs or a bench and a few privacy-giving plants.

EMBRACING GREEN

▶

BAINBRIDGE ISLAND, WA By nature, this garden is mostly shaded and often damp. So the homeowner, a garden designer, chose to focus on foliage, not flowers, for a corner retreat beneath the canopy of native hazelnut and Indian plum trees. She supplemented the native backdrop with an edging of richly textured evergreens, including yellow Japanese forest grass (*Hakonechloa macra* 'Aureola') behind the bench and Japanese sweet flag (*Acorus gramineus* 'Ogon') in the foreground. She also mixed in variegated foliage plants—*Brunnera macrophylla* 'Jack Frost', next to the forest grass, and Tartarian dogwood (*Cornus alba* 'Elegantissima'). Delicate ferns and the big, puckered leaves of *Rodgersia pinnata* add further interest. A lime-colored urn enhances the monochromatic color scheme. **DESIGN** Tish Treherne

LIGHT TOUCH

◀

SAN FRANCISCO Hardy Mediterranean plants give this city garden its sense of serenity. Screens of English laurel (*Prunus laurocerasus*) provide privacy, while a 50-year-old olive tree shades one corner. The key to making all-green plantings interesting, says the designer, is to mix in chartreuse and variegated foliage. Here, green *Choisya ternata* 'Sundance' and *Dietes grandiflora* 'Variegata' brighten the border. Smart plant choices, along with permeable paving, keep this garden drought-tolerant. **DESIGN** Katharine Webster

DECKED OUT

▶

SAN MATEO, CA A stylish wood deck occupies most of this backyard, so the plantings around it are simple and graphic. The L-shaped hedge behind the outdoor sofa—an espaliered *Podocarpus gracilior*—is useful as well; it makes the hot tub hidden behind totally private. And it adds a big jolt of greenery to a backyard that is largely hardscape. Bands of silvery blue *Dymondia margaretae* trace the edge of the deck. **DESIGN** Beth Mullins

BORDERS AT WORK

Plants can provide much more than window dressing for a garden. The right groupings, in the right place, can create soft privacy screening or divide a garden's interior spaces into smaller "rooms."

PRIVACY SCREEN

◄

WEST SEATTLE, WA This beautiful border provides a measure of privacy for the home behind. And because it fringes a corner lot and contains gorgeous shrubs of varied shapes and textures, it's also a neighborhood showstopper. Red-tipped Japanese barberry (*Berberis thunbergii atropurpurea* 'Rose Glow') echoes the rich plum-chocolate hues of the home's trim and anchors the composition, which includes (left to right) green mugo pine; lavender-tipped *Salvia officinalis* 'Purpurascens'; yellow-and-orange-leafed *Nandina domestica* 'Gulf Stream'; yellow-flowered *Euphorbia* 'Blue Haze'; strappy bronze phormium; and pale-yellow-flowered santolina. A pair of skinny yews (*Taxus x media* 'Beanpole') and a big golden Hinoki cypress accent the backdrop. DESIGN Deborah Ellman

ROOM DIVIDER

▼

WEST HOLLYWOOD, CA Shapely drought-tolerant plants create a border between the backyard patio, in the foreground, and a firepit area, behind. A blue-green Weber agave (*Agave weberi*) mimics a cooling fountain above blue *Senecio mandraliscae* in the center, with smaller fox tail agave (*Agave attenuata*) clustered at left. The fuzzy fringe of kangaroo paw blooms (*Anigozanthos* 'Orange Cross') and a lower orange *Echeveria* 'Afterglow' echo the fiery hues of the striped cushions cozying up to the rusted metal fire bowl in back. The patio is of precast concrete pavers; crushed rock covers much of the yard, with a circle of decomposed granite defining the firepit area. DESIGN Eric Brandon Gomez

PATIO PLANTINGS

Paved areas call for simple plantings that provide privacy around them, accent the corners, or tuck neatly between pavers to soften them. Sometimes all three.

COOL POOLSIDE

▲

MENLO PARK, CA Stout lady palms (*Rhapis excelsa*), backed by a gray wall that shows off their shapes, line up like lollipops in a 2-foot-wide raised bed. Steely blue willow wattle (*Acacia iteaphylla*), a slightly weeping shrub, grows in the ground at right next to a green sago palm. Bamboo provides a leafy backdrop. DESIGN Daniel Nolan

RETRO RETREAT

▶

MENLO PARK, CA For gardeners across the West, the word *drought* can be a buzzkill. But this Palm Springs–inspired patio is low on water needs, high in retro style, and sleek and modern to show off the plants. Spare but dramatic plantings include succulents fringing a small water trough; *Yucca recurvifolia* in low bowls on the seat wall; a giant boxed *Agave attenuata* in one corner, and tiny potted cactus on shelves behind the hanging chair. An irregular patchwork of precut pavers juts into a free-form path of decomposed granite. It's an evening garden—a place to lean back in the Acapulco chairs and savor the day's cooling temperatures. DESIGN Lauren Dunec Hoang and Johanna Silver

CITY JUNGLE

▶

SAN FRANCISCO Tiers of greenery turned this pint-size backyard into an oasis. Wispy *Pittosporum tenuifolium* 'Silver Sheen' creates a spatter-paint effect along the fence. On either side, palm grass *(Setaria palmifolia)* sends out bold, fountainlike leaves. Succulents *(Aeonium* 'Jolly Green' and *Agave attenuata)* and grasses (mounding blue *Festuca glauca* 'Elijah Blue' and tufted green mondo grass) fill in the understory. Limiting plant colors to shades of green keeps the space serene (see overview, page 17). DESIGN Beth Mullins

SLOPES

The West's many hills present challenges to gardeners who live on or below them. High on the list: best ways to plant them. You can't till a slope before planting—it will loosen and slide. But you can amend the soil without digging, as the designer of this Northern California garden proves. The right mix of grasses and blooming shrubs covers the slope, creating a living "painting" to view from the patio at its base.

TERRACED HILLSIDE

◄

DANVILLE, CA Unsure that they could accomplish anything with the steep slope behind their home, the owners envied neighbors who had flat lots and pools. Still, they had a vision for their backyard with its narrow, flat patio and nearly vertical hillside beyond: "Palm Springs meets W Hotel style." So the designer painted the retaining walls black to "make them disappear," then added steps and a meandering path across the slope's top. He filled in with drought-tolerant plants. Trailing rosemary spills over the wall on both sides of a gas fireplace.
DESIGN Colin Miller

WATER MUSIC

►

To help camouflage the existing concrete retaining wall at the slope's base, the designer converted a built-in planter into a fountain, lined with a metal trough and edged with ipe wood. Agaves create a fountain effect behind, while upslope yellow kangaroo paws, red penstemons, and various grasses—*Lomandra longifolia* 'Breeze', blue oat grass, *Miscanthus sinensis* 'Morning Light', and deer grass—add color and shimmer.

SLOPE PLANTING

►

Before planting, the designer and his crew covered the slope with jute netting to help control erosion and cut through it to dig planting holes. Then they set wire baskets into each hole to protect the plants' root balls from gophers. Lavender (*Lavandula* x *intermedia* 'Provence') mingles with grasses near the slope's top.

FRONT YARDS

It's easy to love lawns for their lush green color and silky softness beneath bare feet. But in arid climates plagued with recurring droughts, lawns that are planted just to look at don't make sense; most types need too much water to thrive. That's why front yards around the West are now featuring native or locally adapted plants with beautiful and very region-specific results.

SCULPTURE GARDEN

▲

PALM SPRINGS, CA Midcentury modern architecture and the strong shapes of cactus were made for each other, as this desert garden demonstrates. Before the renovation, a lawn covered the front yard, and shrubs hugged the home's walls, obscuring its clean lines. Now, gentle berms covered with sand-colored decomposed granite ripple across the space, imitating the native landscape. And each plant is allotted enough room to show off its sculptural form. Tall columns of *Cereus peruvianus* rise in front of the orange wall, and silver dollar prickly pear (*Opuntia robusta*) fans out its "bunny ears" among golden barrel cactus (*Echinocactus grusonii*). A palo verde tree (*Parkinsonia* 'Desert Museum') and skinny-stemmed lady's slipper (*Pedilanthus macrocarpus*) edge the path. **DESIGN** Desert Landscape Design

LAWN TO LANDSCAPE

▶

VENICE, CA Before the redesign, this 700-square-foot front yard consisted of one mature palm tree and a lawn with a worn pathway from the driveway to the front door. Now it has a proper entrance and just the right balance of privacy and neighborliness. Plants veil the street rather than block it out entirely. They include kangaroo paw (*Anigozanthos* 'Big Red') and threadleaf Japanese maple (*Acer palmatum* 'Seiryu'), right of the path. Feathery *Stipa tenuissima* grass adds motion, and dark flax (*Phormium tenax* 'Bronze') ties the new landscape to the existing purple-leaf plum (*Prunus cerasifera* 'Atropurpurea') in the parkway.
DESIGN Naomi Sanders

BACK TO NATURE

▶

BOULDER, CO Water-wise perennials, many of them native to the mountain region, replaced turf in this front yard. Lavender, red hummingbird trumpet (*Zauschneria arizonica*), mounds of red pineleaf penstemon (*Penstemon pinifolius*), yellow treasure flower (*Gazania linearis*), and ruby muhly grass (*Muhlenbergia reverchonii*) contrast against a compact Colorado spruce tree along a gentle rise. DESIGN Lauren Springer Ogden and Scott Ogden

PATTERNS, COLORS, AND A SENSE OF PLACE

The right plants, in the right place, can turn the simplest gardens into works of art. A splash of golden blooms can add sizzle to a grouping of greens, for instance. Low shrubs with richly textured foliage and seasonal bloom can bring alive an otherwise quiet winter garden. Even grasses can create striking patterns when you tuck them between pavers.

PRAIRIE LIGHTS

▲

BOZEMAN, MT Upright grasses, perennials, and low, mounding shrubs carry the summer show in this garden on the Gallatin River. Swaths of *Rudbeckia fulgida sullivantii* 'Goldsturm' brighten the thriving prairielike planting with sunshiny color, as do the haze of blond seed heads on tufted hair grass (*Deschampsia cespitosa*) and the delicate wands of blue oat grass (*Helictotrichon sempervirens*). Filling in around them are fanlike clumps of Siberian iris (*I. sibirica* 'Caesar's Brother') and compact asters (*A. cordifolius* 'Wood's Purple'). The lawn behind is of 'Durar' hard fescue, a cool-season, drought-tolerant pasture grass, best in mountain regions, that needs very little mowing or feeding. Quaking aspens and cottonwoods provide the green backdrop. **DESIGN** Linda Iverson

PATTERNS
▲

MONTECITO, CA If it weren't for the tracery of California field sedge (*Carex praegracilis*) stitching together the patio and mini meadow, this chaparral-scented garden might look as though planted entirely by nature. But in fact, it's a tailored and richly textured complement to the natural vegetation cloaking the Santa Barbara foothills. And it pairs native plants with equally water-wise Mediterranean plants, including lavender beside the wall at right; mounding *Salvia greggii* 'Alba', center; rosemary spilling over the wall; and woolly thyme creating a tapestry effect between pavers on the far patio. Native plants cloaking the hillside include bay, oak, toyon, and California white sage (*Salvia apiana*). The sedge (*Carex*) meadow can be mown to look like a lawn, but needs much less water.
DESIGN Susan Van Atta

SENSE OF PLACE
▶

BAINBRIDGE ISLAND, WA Forest green and water blue are the Pacific Northwest's most natural hues. But under soft blue or leaden skies, shrubs that bloom are welcome additions. Here, a *Euphorbia characias wulfenii* forms a mound of silvery blue foliage between blue grama (*Bouteloua gracilis*), whose blond seed heads rise in front, and fluffy green eulalia grass (*Miscanthus sinensis*). In summer, the leafy planting looks quiet, as though planted by nature on the edge of Puget Sound. But in late spring, the euphorbia sends up clusters of sunny yellow blooms.

CHAPTER

2

Beds and Borders

CLASSICAL
▶

Bear's breech (*Acanthus mollis*) commands attention for its bold, architectural foliage. It also has spectacular summer flowers. In this Seattle garden, it is paired with a feathery grass.

OUT OF THE BOX
◀

Silvery sea kale (*Crambe maritima*) sprawls on rocky shores in the wild, so it looks right at home inching its way onto gravel in a Hillsboro, Oregon, garden. Behind it is black mondo grass (*Ophiopogon planiscapus* 'Nigrescens'). A tall clump of reed grass (*Calamagrostis brachytricha*) and a blue cedar (*Cedrus deodara* 'Divinely Blue') are to the left.
DESIGN Laura Crockett

Beds and borders are made interesting by the types of plants they contain and the way those plants work together. Take design cues from your region's natural vegetation, the climate, the exposure (sun or shade), and your home's style. Before heading to the nursery, pick a color theme, whether shades of green, or blues and coral. Then choose plants in a range of heights, shapes, and sizes—from upright columns to soft mounds to flat mats—that carry it out. Vary leaf sizes and textures too. Incorporate some small evergreen shrubs to give the border structure from season to season.

VERTICAL

Feather reed grass (*Calamagrostis* x *acutiflora* 'Karl Forester') is an ideal plant for narrow spaces, as its growth habit is very erect. In this Pleasant Hill, California, garden, its flower stems soar well above the wall, where they provide a wispy outdoor room divider.
DESIGN Joseph Huettl

SHOWSTOPPER

If you have the space and love color, indulge yourself. Plant a border made up almost entirely of shrubs. With so many choices on the market, you can create a dramatic border based almost entirely on colorful foliage as pictured here, in *Sunset*'s garden in Menlo Park, California, and have it look good for much of the year. Mostly foliage borders mean that maintenance is a cinch.

GOLD RUSH

◄

Golden foliage plays a major part in the border, shown here from the end opposite the cordyline. Variegated *Cistus corbariensis* 'Little Miss Sunshine' forms a golden mound in the foreground, where it covers itself with cheerful white flowers in spring. Clumps of blue fescue (*Festuca glauca* 'Beyond Blue') to its right cool the heat of the red-tinged *Nandina domestica* 'Obsession' and bronze-tinged *Abelia* 'Kaleidoscope'. Across the path, brilliant *Carex oshimensis* 'Everillo' and blue pots filled with *Nandina domestica* 'Lemon-Lime' cool things off a bit. At the very back is an imposing *Phormium* 'Black Adder'.

SPLASHES OF WINE

►

Grasslike *Cordyline* 'Design-a-Line Burgundy' and plum-hued *Loropetalum chinense* 'Purple Pixie' add drama to the front of this wide border. Bright gold *Carex oshimensis* 'Everillo', at left, and silvery *Astelia chathamica x nervosa* 'Silver Shadow', behind the cordyline, provide contrast. Midway back, an apricot-flowered *Digiplexis* 'Illumination Flame' echoes the fiery hues of heavenly bamboo (*Nandina domestica* 'Obsession') toward the back.
DESIGN Janet Sluis, Johanna Silver, and Lauren Dunec Hoang

CORDYLINE 'DESIGN-A-LINE BURGUNDY' This fine-textured cordyline hybrid grows 2 to 3 feet tall and as wide and has an attractive weeping form. It is an excellent container plant as well as a border accent.

CISTUS CORBARIENSIS 'LITTLE MISS SUNSHINE' Rockrose (*Cistus*) is a bulletproof plant—salt-tolerant, heat-tolerant, drought-tolerant. This new variety also sports very showy leaves with a green center stripe and bright gold edges. It stays short, 12 inches tall, spreading to about 18 inches.

DIGIPLEXIS 'ILLUMINATION FLAME' This flashy perennial is a cross between foxglove (*Digitalis*) and a near cousin (*Isoplexis*), a shrub from the Canary Islands. Its flowers have yellow-orange throats and fuchsia edges. Because the plant is sterile, it blooms over a long season—spring well into fall.

WOODSY

If you live close to wildland, you might want a garden that looks as if you did not have a hand in it at all. A garden that seems to have happened spontaneously rather than one that's been meticulously plotted. Nature, just a tad neater. Relying primarily on simple foliage is the key to achieving this look.

RAIN FOREST
◄

Japanese sweet flag (*Acorus gramineus* 'Ogon'), the gold-leafed, grassy plants on both sides of this Bainbridge Island, Washington, creekbed, likes boggy soil and thrives in wet, shady gardens. Blue hostas (*H.* 'Halcyon') and ferns—*Polystichum munitum* in front of the hosta, *P. makinoi* behind—are perfect partners along the creekbed. An existing native hazel tree (*Corylus cornuta x californica*) provides shade. DESIGN Tish Treherne

CLOUD COVER
◄

A mass planting of evergreen miscanthus (*M. transmorrisonensis*), billowing between jacaranda trees (*J. mimosifolia*), edges this patio in Palo Alto, California. When the grasses are in bloom, they shimmer like blond clouds. A fringe of wisteria grows against the wall at right. DESIGN Andrea Cochran

WOODLAND RETREAT
▶

Coral bark maple (*Acer palmatum* 'Sango Kaku') rises behind a seating area in a Bainbridge Island, Washington, garden. Its leaves are bright green in summer, turning gold in fall, and its bark, twigs, and branches become bright coral in winter. It is paired here with ferns—bracken (*Pteridium aquilinum*) on the left and Western five-finger fern (*Adiantum aleuticum*) on the right—plus yellow-flowered *Ranunculus hispidus*. DESIGN Cassie Picha

ZEN STYLE

Japanese gardens are compatible with Western style. Their emphasis on a natural look, even if a stylized version, appeals to the Western fondness of the outdoors. And their minimalism complements contemporary architecture. Such serenity is also a good antidote to overscheduled, multitasking lives.

FOCUS ON FLOWERS

▼

Though there are only three flowering plants in this Palo Alto, California, garden, the dwarf pink kangaroo paws (*Anigozanthos* 'Pink Joey') are the center of attention because of their placement against a blank white wall. Understated foliage plants make up the rest of the garden: on this side of the fence, variegated *Pittosporum tenuifolium* 'Marjorie Channon' and the darker green *P. t.* 'Silver Sheen'; on the other, a towering bamboo (*Bambusa malingensis*). DESIGN Stefan Thuilot

SUPER NATURAL

▶

This planting in Portland is artfully casual—a few columns of Italian cypress (*Cupressus sempervirens*), several mounds of *Libertia ixioides* 'Goldfinger', and, for seasonal interest, a spot of feather reed grass (*Calamagrostis x acutiflora* 'Karl Foerster'). The finish of the simple metal firepit suggests a rustic campfire, but its elegant shape evokes Japanese sculpture.
DESIGN Annie Bamberger

SCREEN PAINTING

▼

The beautiful form of weeping blue Atlas cedar (*Cedrus atlantica* 'Glauca Pendula') deserves a bare wall behind it to show off its silhouette. All the other plants in this Hayden Island, Oregon, garden, which include bracken fern, vinca, Scotch moss, and garden geranium, were kept lower than the tree's canopy so as not to compete.

GREEN SCREEN

▶

Horsetail (*Equisetum hyemale*) lining the walls of a Palos Verdes, California, courtyard garden creates the same neutral green effect that a screening of bamboo would, but in much less space. Ribbons of woolly thyme (*Thymus serpyllum*) soften the hardscape along with pocket plantings of two succulents: *Agave attenuata* and *A. parryi*. DESIGN Jim Lord

QUIET OUTBURSTS

◀

Three evergreen plants of similar habit but different colors and textures add interest to a patio entrance in a Santa Monica garden. In front are two variegated sweet flags—golden *Acorus gramineus* 'Ogon' and white-striped *A. g.* 'Variegatus'. Springing up behind them (at left) is asparagus fern (*Asparagus densiflorus*). DESIGN Gabriela Yariv

YIN AND YANG

▶

The pale color and weeping shape of *Carex morrowii* 'Silver Sceptre' edging this Portland border provide a soft contrast to the dark, dense hedge behind it—*Euonymus japonica* 'Green Spire'. A variegated *Pittosporum tenuifolium* 'Marjorie Channon' acts as mediator. DESIGN Lauren Hall-Behrens

AGING BEAUTIFULLY

▶

A trio of shade plants—ostrich fern (*Matteuccia struthiopteris*), upright wild ginger (*Saruma henryi*) tucked behind it, and strappy snowdrop (*Galanthus*)—fill a shady garden corner in Portland. Echoing all the greens, a spot of moss tops the stone toadstool nestled among them. DESIGN Annie Bamberger

DROUGHT-PROOF COLOR

▶

Waves of French lavender (*Lavandula intermedia* 'Grosso') carry the show in this Hollywood Hills, California, garden, along with blond grasses. Cleveland sage (*Salvia clevelandii*) and chartreuse-flowered *Euphorbia characias wulfenii* in the background repeat the yellow and blue color scheme. Silver *Artemisia* 'Powis Castle' adds sparkle.
DESIGN Judy Kameon

PERFECT PAIR

◀

A hedge of green germander (*Teucrium chamaedrys*) frames a billowy smoke bush (*Cotinus coggygria* 'Royal Purple') on this gentle slope in Dayton, Oregon. Both are at their best when slightly stressed; they actually prefer poor, rocky soil and irrigation on the light side.
DESIGN Jacqueline Authier

SUN-PROOF

◀

A shocking pink *Cordyline* 'Electric Pink' fans out its glowing leaves in front of a variegated star of Madeira (*Echium candicans* 'Variegata') in a San Diego garden. Both plants do best in full sun.

MEDITERRANEAN

With their mild, rainy winters and warm, dry summers, Mediterranean climates such as those in California and much of the Southwest are lovely to live in. But gardening can be challenging, especially during periods of prolonged drought. Your best bet is to choose pretty plants that thrive on little summer water—those that evolved here (or in one of the world's other dry summer climates). Many have waxy, fuzzy, velvety, or succulent leaves that help them flourish on very little water. Lavender, cistus, rosemary, *Santolina*, and *Westringia*, along with many grasses, groundcovers, and trees, are examples.

TUSCANY IN CALIFORNIA
▲

A low clipped hedge of germander (*Teucrium chamaedrys*) edges a bed of clipped rosemary and balls of gray *Westringia glabra* next to wildland in Ojai, California. The quintessential Mediterranean garden is all about foliage, often neatly pruned. The nearest tree is a black mission fig, surrounded by a clipped pomegranate hedge. The trees in the background are coast live oaks.
DESIGN Paul Hendershot

LAVENDER AND LEMONS
◄

Eureka lemons add sunshiny fruits to a Palo Alto, California, garden. The tree is underplanted with Spanish lavender (*Lavandula stoechas* 'Otto Quast') and gray-leafed California fuchsia (*Zauschneria californica*), a native. Woolly thyme (*Thymus serpyllum*) flanks the border and softens the path.

SERENELY SIMPLE
▶

A neatly pruned hedge of germander (*Teucrium chamaedrys*) and three balls of clipped dwarf myrtle (*Myrtus communis tarentina* 'Compacta') edge the gravel patio in this Ojai, California, garden. The few other carefully selected plants include a Cécile Brünner rose that climbs the stone wall, and an olive tree.
DESIGN Paul Hendershot

TIPS from a PRO

Santa Barbara–based landscape designer **MARGIE GRACE** has created gardens in many dry climates, including Spain, Australia, and the Southwest. "A dry garden can be lush, sculptural, artsy," she says. Here's how she adds pizzazz to plantings.

COLOR

Use shrubs such as lavender, rosemary, and thyme for showy flowers during the warm season. Look for color on leaves—silver and blue-gray foliage butting against deep green.

LIGHT AND MOTION

Mix in a few blond grasses (like slender veldt grass) that shimmer in sunlight and dance in breezes.

OPEN SPACES

Leave pockets of the garden unplanted. Dress them with pretty mulches such as California gold gravel, then top them with sandstone boulders, a shapely urn, or a tiny recirculating fountain hugged by a few plants. "It's not a compromise to have fewer plants."

PLAYFUL TEXTURES

◄

Two rings of *Santolina*—clipped, gray *S. chamae-cyparissus* and green *S. rosmarinifolia* dotted with little yellow button flowers—create an amusing focal point in a Bolinas, California, garden. English wallflower (*Erysimum* 'Bowles Mauve'), blooming exuberantly, adds contrasting color and form nearby.

MINI MEDITERRANEAN

►

No garden is too small to create a Mediterranean flavor. This patio in Corona del Mar, California, manages it with just an olive tree and an underplanting of *Dianella revoluta* 'Little Rev', plus a trio of olive jars.
DESIGN Chris Fenmore

LUSH CORNER

►

A rich assortment of colors and textures, partially in a border and partially in a planter, creates an inviting space for a solo hangout in a Los Angeles garden. The dark red of kangaroo paw flowers (*Anigozanthos* 'Red Cross') echoes the dark red hues of *Phormium* 'Dusky Chief' in back. The gray-green leaves of dwarf olive (*Olea europaea* 'Little Ollie') complement both plants, as does the splash of *Helichrysum petiolare* 'Limelight' cascading from the planter.
DESIGN Judy Kameon

⩍ Design Element ⩍
FRAGRANCE

Whether sultry, spicy, fruity, or floral, fragrance enhances a garden's romantic mood. To add it, first choose from the universally loved light florals like jasmine, citrus, and rose, and concentrate those plants around decks and patios.

Then use aromatic plants along paths leading to more hidden parts of the garden. Pack creeping thyme between pavers where it will release its scent when stepped on. Use rosemary and divine lavenders for hedges.

For the final delight, add plants that force you to get close before revealing their scent, such as mock orange *(Philadelphus)* for the jasmine perfume of its blooms. Or set a pot of heavenly, heady tuberoses beside a garden bench to enjoy on moonlit nights.

Fragrance isn't essential, of course. But it can turn a garden from ordinary to enchanting.

SUMMER PERFUME

Rows of English lavender (*Lavandula angustifolia*), the hardiest and most widely planted species, stripe the gently rolling fields at this farm near Silverton, Oregon. The best time to enjoy the flowers' fragrance from nearby lawn chairs is just before peak bloom in early summer.

BLUE MOOD

▶

The blue-gray foliage in this Rancho Palos Verdes, California, garden grabs your attention first. It includes blue fescue (*Festuca glauca* 'Elijah Blue'), the small succulent *Oscularia deltoides*, and woolly thyme (*Thymus serpyllum*). The paler yellows and peaches are a subtle complement to the blues. The flowers are *Achillea millefolium* 'Terra Cotta' and the blond grass *Stipa tenuissima*. Caveat: This grass can be invasive in wetter climates; use with caution. DESIGN Tish Treherne

CLOSE HARMONY

◀

The primary color in this Bolinas, California, border is green, provided by the fescue meadow and native shrubs including currant (*Ribes sanguineum*), manzanita (*Arctostaphylos* 'Pacific Mist'), and several varieties of *Ceanothus*. Big splashes of chartreuse *Euphorbia characias wulfenii* and *E. rigida* enliven the composition, as does a scattering of blue-gray foliage courtesy of *Festuca idahoensis* and *Artemisia* 'Powis Castle'. DESIGN Mary Scott

PASTEL MEADOW

◀

Two soft-colored grasses provide most of the interest in a meadow at Denver Botanic Gardens—blue oat grass (*Helictotrichon sempervirens* 'Saphirsprudel') and yellow-green Japanese forest grass (*Hakonechloa macra* 'Aureola'). The white-flowering yarrow (*Achillea millefolium*) adds texture without altering the gentle color scheme.

REFINED RUSTIC

If you live somewhere near wildland, or you just want a landscape that looks like wildland, resist the manicured look. Use gentle curved lines instead of strong graphic patterns and subtle rather than bold colors.

THE LATE SHOW

▲

Late summer is often the showiest season in New Mexico as this Santa Fe garden proves. Blue grama (*Bouteloua gracilis*) and other grasses, studded with yellow coneflowers (*Ratibida pinnata*) and mounds of the annual purple native hoary aster (*Dieteria canascens*), ramble beneath a New Mexican privet (*Forestiera neomexicana*) cloaked in golden fall leaves. DESIGN Donna Bone

STYLED
WILD

If you want a garden that looks a bit wild, but you want to show off a little too, keep the outlines soft but go bolder with plant shapes, accents, and the color scheme.

MEDITERRANEAN MIX

▲

This Tucson garden looks distinctly "deserty," but only the *Agave parryi truncata*, at center, and the yellow-flowered blackfoot daisy (*Melampodium leucanthum*), up front, are Arizona natives. The rest of the plants, from Mediterranean climates, include chartreuse-flowered *Euphorbia rigida*, lavender, *Aloe ferox*, and the blond grass.
DESIGN Elizabeth Przygoda-Montgomery

BANISH THE BOUNDARIES

You don't have to live in a rural area to have a wild garden. You just need to loosen up a little. In this Northern California garden, spiky plants—silvery *Astelia nivicola* 'Red Gem' and rosy *Cordyline* 'Electric Pink'—look as though they have escaped from a nearby border to settle themselves in a patch of "no-mow fescue." Large succulents in the loose border behind—green *Agave attenuata* and gray-purple *Echeveria* 'Afterglow'—repeat the same silvery and red tones, as do the *Leucadendron* 'Summer Red', at right, and *L.* 'Safari Sunset', at left.
DESIGN Reynolds-Sebastiani

GOING NATIVE

Using native plants that grow together in the wild will create a natural-looking garden. All the plants will inevitably seem as if they belong together. You can create the same nature-planted effect with non-natives, as long as you give them a natural-looking setting, as shown opposite.

MOSTLY NATIVE
◀

The planting in this mostly native San Leandro, California, garden includes blue-flowered *Salvia leucophylla*, white-flowered *Achillea millefolium*, shrubby vine hill manzanita (*Arctostaphylos densiflora*), and coast live oaks. The only import is the grass, *Festuca rubra* 'Molate'.
DESIGN Michael Thilgen

NATIVE IN SPIRIT
▶

Apricot-flowered sunroses (*Helianthemum nummularium* 'Cheviot') look perfectly at home beside a Scotch pine (*Pinus sylvestris* 'Albyn Prostrata') and blue fescue (*Festuca glauca*) in a Bainbridge Island, Washington, garden. The extensive use of stone contributes to the natural look, suggesting that the plants sprang up around outcroppings all on their own.
DESIGN Tish Treherne

SINGING THE BLUES

Blue flowers—whether sky blue or cobalt blue—are not as abundant in the plant kingdom as, say, orange and yellow. Violets, red-violets, lavenders, and lilacs abound, but blues that don't lean toward red are rare. Still, they are out there, and many are native to the West.

Foothill penstemon (*P. heterophyllus*), pictured, is one of those good blues. *P.* 'Margarita BOP' blooms are sky blue, fading to purple. Blue-eyed grass (*Sisyrinchium bellum*), a small perennial in the iris family, unfurls charming light blue flowers in spring, while blue flax (*Linum lewisii*) bears light blue flowers atop wispy stems (pretty among ornamental grasses).

Among unthirsty, blue-flowered shrubs are various species of California lilac (*Ceanothus*). Those with the bluest flowers, which appear in late winter or spring, include *Ceanothus gloriosus* 'Anchor Bay'; *C. griseus horizontalis* 'Yankee Point' (medium blue); *C.* 'Concha' (dark blue), one of the best for gardens; *C.* 'Dark Star' (dark cobalt blue); *C.* 'Joyce Coulter' (medium blue); and *C.* 'Julia Phelps' (dark indigo).

Among non-native, true blues are forget-me-nots (*Myosotis sylvatica*); dwarf plumbago (*Ceratostigma plumbaginoides*); and a number of salvias, all drought-tolerant, including *S. chamaedryoides*, *S. guaranitica*, *S. patens*, *S. sinaloensis*, *S.* 'Costa Rica Blue', and *S.* 'Indigo Spires'.

⩧ *Design Element* ⩧
TOUCH

Humans are born with the urge to explore through the sense of touch. You never outgrow that impulse, so why not indulge it? A garden provides the perfect opportunity. Just add some plants whose foliage or flowers are simply irresistible.

The spongy, peeling bark of a *Melaleuca* tree begs to be touched; so does a palo verde's silky-smooth trunk, and the caressable flowers of bottlebrush (*Callistemon*).

The woolly white leaves of dusty miller (*Senecio cineraria*) are hard to resist. So are the whisper-light plumes of pink muhly (*Muhlenbergia capillaris*) and the feathery seed heads of Apache plume (*Fallugia paradoxa*) and *Pennisetum massaicum* 'Red Bunny Tails'.

Creating a touch-me garden couldn't be easier. Just use your hands at the nursery.

PURE VELVET

Thick, silvery leaves of lamb's ears *(Stachys byzantina)* are cloaked with fine hairs that create a furry effect—kitten-soft to touch. The plants form dense, ground-hugging rosettes, perfect for the fronts of borders.

FEATHERY

One species, planted en masse, can be enough to create a stunning
border, especially if the plants have foliage or blooms that make you
want to reach out and touch them.

FALL FIREWORKS
◄

Pink muhly grass (*Muhlenbergia capillaris*) is a small, dark green mound most of the year, but it doubles its size with airy plumes of feathery red flowers in fall. Cut back this grass in late winter for new growth in spring. Pink muhly is very drought-tolerant, but looks better and grows larger with some supplemental water.

HAWAIIAN HEDGE
►

For most of the world, croton (*Codiaeum variegatum*) is a houseplant or summer annual. But in Hawaii, it grows easily into a tall shrub. This exuberant hedge edges a driveway in Kona, on the Big Island.

ELEGANT FRINGE
►

Variegated Japanese sedge (*Carex morrowii* 'Variegata') edges both sides of this long, sweeping border in a Vancouver, Washington, garden. The darker, denser holly (*Ilex x meserveae* 'Blue Boy') planted between them sets off the sedge's graceful shape and near-white color.

WISPY

Some plants are so delicate in appearance, it seems a mere whisper would set them in motion. Using these airy plants lavishly accents their kinetic nature and creates a mesmerizing effect, especially when they ripple in the lightest breeze.

FLECKS

▶

Coral flowers of humming-bird mint (*Agastache*) give this garden in Vancouver, Washington, an airy appearance. They resemble kernels of popped corn on a stem against a delicate blue backdrop formed by *Lavandula* x *intermedia* 'Provence'. DESIGN Karen Ford

PLUMES

◀

The silver-beige flower plumes of *Pennisetum* 'Fairy Tails' and Atlas fescue (*Festuca mairei*) sway readily in the slightest breeze, but their slope-side location in this Danville, California, garden assures they are in near-constant motion. Fine-textured germander (*Teucrium* x *lucidrys*), at left, with red-purple blooms, continues the delicate mood at the top of the hill. Stalks of yellow kangaroo paw (*Anigozanthos* 'Bush Gold') add some counterbalancing heft. DESIGN Stefan Thuilot

TENDRILS

▶

Tillandsia (air plants) on a tree branch create living wall art in a Laguna Beach, California, garden. The rosettes are firmly attached to tails of Spanish moss (another type of tillandsia) that are draped over the branch so they move in the breeze. Mother-in-law's tongue (*Sansevieria trifasciata*), which is normally a houseplant but can be grown outdoors where winters are mild, fills the narrow border below. DESIGN Dustin Gimbel

LACY

Small-flowered plants look more substantial when several are planted together and their colors intermingle. As happens when you look at a piece of lace, you focus on the pattern and not on the open spaces in between.

APRICOT LACE
◀

Achillea millefolium 'Terra Cotta' mingles with slender stems of thatching reed (*Thamnochortus insignis*) in a backyard meadow in Rancho Palos Verdes, California. The grass is flexible enough to vibrate in the wind; you almost expect to hear it hum like a tuning fork.
DESIGN Tish Treherne

BLUE CONFETTI

◄

Cornflowers (*Centaurea cyanus*) scatter bits of color against a backdrop of blond meadow grasses, including moor grass (*Molina caerulea*), in Sheridan, Oregon. Because this annual is tall and delicate, its flowers make beautiful accents among meadow grasses.

PURPLE FROTH

▲

Waves of color weave across an Albion, California, slope in a design reminiscent of a pointillist painting. The purple is courtesy of English lavender (*Lavandula angustifolia*). The rest of the colors come from grasses: pink *Pennisetum advena* 'Rubrum' and, in the background, green *Calamagrostis brachytricha*. DESIGN Gary Ratway

VELVETY

Some plants beg to be touched; their leaves are silky or velvety, or soft and fuzzy. Others, such as the feathery seed heads of ornamental grasses, create "visual velvet." They produce a soft cloud of color that, especially when viewed from a distance, makes you want to reach out and caress them. Plant your favorite touchables toward the front of borders where they're within easy reach.

MISTY WAVES
▼

Ribbons of soft color bathe a hillside planting at Oakwood Gardens in Hillsboro, Oregon. The russet wave in front is meadowsweet (*Filipendula palmata*); the rosy one above it is switch grass (*Panicum virgatum* 'Shenandoah'). At the top of the hill is a pink cloud of *Eupatorium*. The upright puffs of lavender-blue flowers are Russian sage (*Perovskia atriplicifolia*). DESIGN Lucy Hardiman and Laura Crockett

BETTER THAN SUEDE
▶

Lamb's ears (*Stachys byzantina* 'Big Ears') edges a border in Menlo Park, California, while gray-leafed *Westringia* 'Wynyabbie Gem' adds its soft leaf textures behind two coneflowers—*Echinacea purpurea* 'PowWow Wild Berry' and *E.* 'Sunrise'. Other flowers include rusty-hued *Sedum* 'Autumn Joy' and *Achillea* 'Moonshine' purple *Salvia buchananii* 'Wendy's Wish', and *Penstemon* 'Arabesque Violet'. All plants need little water once established. DESIGN Lauren Dunec Hoang and Johanna Silver

TIPS from a PRO

As test garden designer at *Sunset* in Menlo Park, California, **LAUREN DUNEC HOANG** creates gardens and plantings for the cameras. Here's how she builds small borders.

ESTABLISH STRUCTURE

Shrubs, especially evergreens with interesting shapes, provide the bones of a border and a backdrop for perennial flowers. They also keep the border's form intact in winter, after perennials have died back.

CREATE CONTINUITY

Repeat leaf color and flower color, or clusters of a single plant variety, throughout the border to unify the design. Go for flowers in the same color family—shades of pink, for example. Add flowers in complementary hues like creamy white.

EDGE IT

Set clusters of low, mounding plants such as lamb's ears and coral bells across the front of the border to unify the planting.

DESERT ESSENTIAL

◄

Texas ranger *(Leucophyllum frutescens* 'Compacta') is worth growing just for its lovely leaves, which are densely covered with fine, silvery hair and feel soft as felt. But it has attractive flowers too; they're usually triggered by summer rains in the Southwest deserts. This evergreen shrub (to 5 feet tall), native to the Southwest and northern Mexico, tolerates heat, wind, and alkaline soil. It makes a pretty informal hedge for dry-country gardens.

Design Element
SHAPE

Something magical happens when you combine plants to accentuate their differences. Globes and mounds of foliage with pyramids and columns, for example.

Globes are workhorse perennials and shrubs that make up most gardens. Compact *Pittosporum tobira* 'Wheeler's Dwarf', fountainlike sword ferns, and mounding dwarf conifers are examples. Their friendly contours create perfect drifts in borders.

Then there are cylinders and arrow-straight columns, including some junipers and organpipe cactus (*Stenocereus thurberi*); conical shapes such as dwarf Alberta spruce (*Picea glauca albertiana* 'Conica'); and fan-shaped plants such as New Zealand flax and yucca. All add drama to a planting. Use them to counterbalance round, vertical, and matlike plants.

GLOBES AND FRIENDS

This border, nestled under a pear tree in a Carnation, Washington, garden, is a symphony of shapes, from flattish to upright to rounded. From left to right: weeping, yellow-green Japanese forest grass (*Hakonechloa macra* 'Aureola'); upright pink-flowered Japanese anemone (*Anemone hupehensis japonica* 'Prinz Heinrich'); *Pulmonaria* 'Margery Fish', which forms low mounds of green leaves dappled with silver; threadlike black mondo grass (*Ophiopogon planiscapus* 'Nigrescens'); and twin globes of clipped boxwood (*Buxus sempervirens*). In back, tall *Gladiolus gandavensis* 'Boone' and orange *Dahlia* 'Moonfire' add seasonal interest. DESIGN Daniel Mount

BOLD

It only takes a handful of plants with varied shapes to make a bold statement in borders. Another way to be bold is by growing something more ordinary, such as ornamental grasses, but in a very unexpected way.

CHORUS LINE
◄

A trio of amber-green, cone-shaped arborvitae (*Thuja occidentalis* 'Rheingold') appears to dance around a triangular white fir (*Abies concolor*) in this McMinnville, Oregon, garden. Taller trees behind include columns of green *Thuja* 'Smaragd' midway back and a towering white birch (*Betula pendula*). A few horizontals—a mahogany-hued Japanese maple and a pink rhododendron—fill out the center.

SUMMER DRAMA
◄

Leaves of *Gunnera tinctoria* are seasonal, completely dying back to the ground in winter in most climates. But in summer, the plants send up 4-to-6-foot stalks topped with big leaves that unfurl to form giant cups with frilly edges. *Gunnera* is most effective near pools or next to a short, fine-textured groundcover, as used here in a Bainbridge Island, Washington, garden.

BEAUTIFUL WEEPERS
►

Any one of these pendulous trees would create a dramatic focal point. But using three together, each a different color, as was done in this Silverton, Oregon, garden, is downright theatrical. The trees, from left to right, are *Cupressus arizonica* x *glabra* 'Raywood's Weeping', *Cedrus deodara* 'Gold Cascade', and *Picea engelmannii* 'Bush's Lace'.

SCENE STEALERS

Burgundy foliage is a very useful garden tool. Because it is the opposite of green, the most common color in any garden, wherever you place it burgundy will call attention to itself as well as anything immediately around it.

PERFECT PARTNERS
◄

It is hard to say which plant is more captivating in this section of the Albers Vista Gardens in Bremerton, Washington—the green- and red-leafed sourwood (*Oxydendrum arboreum*) at right, draped with white flower panicles, or the big, mounding sweep of rosy-purple *Berberis thunbergii* 'Rose Glow' to its left. The other attention seeker is serviceberry (*Amelanchier arborea*) in the distance, cloaked in yellow-orange fall leaves. DESIGN John Albers

DARK BEAUTY
▶

No matter how lushly a garden is planted, a dark burgundy fountain of leaves is going to stand out. Here, a pineapple flower (*Eucomis* 'Sparkling Burgundy') accents a soft planting of low, green *Leptinella squalida* and the red-tipped grass *Imperata cylindrica* 'Rubra'. Green *Epimedium grandiflorum* 'Queen Esta', poking through the *Eucomis,* and *Hydrangea* 'Lady in Red', in back, complete this Portland planting. DESIGN Nick Erickson

EYE-CATCHER
▶

Dark-leafed *Phormium* 'Maori Sunrise' spills out beneath a yellow-flowered angel's trumpet (*Brugmansia versicolor* 'Charles Grimaldi') in a Berkeley garden. A variegated *Plectranthus argentatus* grows at its left, and *Phygelius* 'Sunshine' peeks through in back. DESIGN Marcia Donahue

TEXTURES

The softness of ferns, the stiffness of conifers, the fleshy feel of succulents, the glossy polish of hostas—these are just a few of the many foliage textures available. Play up their differences by combining rough leaves with smooth ones, feathery beside frilly, prickly with smooth, to create borders with real wow power.

THREE GRACES
▼

In this section of a Bremerton, Washington, garden the striking differences in foliage color keep the scene lively. A bright green Japanese maple (*Acer palmatum dissectum* 'Viridis'; middle) contrasts with other maples—burgundy 'Inaba Shidare', and, to its right, 'Oshio beni'. The gold mound is *Chamaecyparis pisifera filifera* 'Mops'. Dwarf conifers and sedum encircle the Chinese lantern. DESIGN John Albers, Albers Vista Gardens

SHORT SUBJECTS

▲

Dwarf conifers have wonderful knobby textures that show off well in this section of the Albers Vista Gardens in Bremerton, Washington. The front row includes (left to right) two spruce trees (*Picea glehnii* 'Chitosemaru' and *P. abies* 'Pusch') and two fir trees (*Abies grandis* 'Van Dedem's Dwarf' and *A. nordmanniana* 'Hunnewell Broom'). A dwarf *Pieris* (*P. japonica* 'Bonsai Adromeda') grows on the far left. The bright blooms and open habit of *Santolina virens* 'Lemon Fizz' in the background are a good foil for the denseness of the conifers. Pink-flowering *Sempervivum* brightens the foreground.
DESIGN John Albers

GREEN PLUMES

▲

With its big, fan-shaped leaves and bright green color, ostrich fern (*Matteuccia struthiopteris*) looks almost tropical. But it is very hardy and does better in colder locations, such as this garden in Denver, than in milder ones. Its companions are *Spiraea* 'Limemound' and a potted Japanese maple.

TANGLED WOODS

A dwarf false cypress, planted in multiples in Battle Ground, Washington, has magnificently complex foliage—droopy branchlets with stringy foliage—and a bright golden yellow color to boot. Its botanical name, *Chamaecyparis pisifera filifera* 'Mops', is almost as complicated.

BEAUTIFUL EDGES

Where a lawn, meadow, or path meets up with a border, you need to consider what you want that intersection to look like. Random curves softened by sprawling plants can work in informal gardens, but defined edges usually create a more elegant look next to mat-forming groundcovers.

REINED IN

▶

A raised bed, enclosed in Cor-ten steel and planted with blue moor grass (*Sesleria caerulea*), creates a very clean line between lawn and border in a Palo Alto, California, garden. The walkway of pavers, interplanted with turf, further emphasizes the border's geometric pattern. Paperbark maple trees (*Acer griseum*) are accents. DESIGN Stefan Thuilot

CONTINUOUS CASCADE

◀

The contours of this Woodside, California, border are deeply curved, and all the plants along its edge have rounded shapes as well: the bronze *Carex testacea*, at center; the bright green *Thymus x citriodorus* 'Lime', to its left; and the big *Miscanthus transmorrisonensis*, topped with pink plumes, at far left. A single *Yucca recurvifolia* and three clumps of spiky *Phormium* 'Platt's Black', plus the bold, gray-green *Melianthus major*, add some starch to balance all the softness. DESIGN Chris Jacobson

GRASS ON GRASS

▶

Unmowed *Festuca rubra* edges this border in a Los Altos, California, garden. Taller *Miscanthus sinensis*, topped with rust-colored seed heads, continues the play of fine textures in mid-border, while purple leaf plum (*Prunus cerasifera*) and French lavender add variety. DESIGN Arterra Landscape Architects

TRANSITIONS

Borders that transition from one color palette to another or from formal to casual moods need something to bridge the gap. It could be plants with complex variegation, or objects such as a large urn, garden sculpture, or big boulders. They are a signal it is time to stop and change gears.

CALM TO EXUBERANT

◀

Two chunky boulders mark the transition between low-growing, inky black mondo grass (*Ophiopogon planiscapus* 'Nigrescens') and lime *Sedum rupestre* 'Angelina' and the taller, more exuberant plants behind in this ever-changing border in Seattle. *Rudbeckia fulgida sullivantii* 'Goldsturm' displays its golden blooms in summer, beside mounds of brown *Carex tenuiculmis* 'Cappuccino'. The gray mound in front with a single copper bloom is sunrose (*Helianthemum* x *nummularium* 'Henfield Brilliant'). It puts on its main show in spring or early summer. The spots of reddish pink are *Calluna vulgaris* 'Firefly', which changes color with the season. DESIGN Stacie Crooks

WARM TO COOL

▲

A large jade green urn, fringed at its base with a nearly matching dwarf *Cedrus deodara* 'Feelin' Blue', marks the spot where this Bainbridge Island, Washington, border shifts from plants of warm golds and bronzes to soft neutral greens. Chartreuse *Sedum rupestre* 'Angelina' grows in front of the container; its spent brown flowers have been left in place to complement the grasses. The tall grass behind the container is *Miscanthus sinensis* 'Morning Light'. DESIGN Tish Treherne

MASTER MIXER

Although coral bells (*Heuchera*) produce delicate spikes of tiny, bell-shaped blooms in spring, its leaves come in a fantastic array of colors, most marbled and/or veined with a second or third color. 'Lime Rickey' has cool chartreuse leaves and makes a striking edging for darker green foliage plants in lightly shaded borders. 'Southern Comfort' has big, maplelike leaves in a shade of burnt caramel; it's pretty beside tawny grasses. 'Persian Carpet' has silver leaves with dark purple veins, and 'Chocolate Veil' has brown leaves with light purple and silver marbling. Try 'Mahogany' (pictured) with a coppery *Carex* and a lime *Spiraea*.

ENERGY SOURCES

Including one plant that looks as if it wants to skyrocket to the heavens adds excitement to any border—even a small planting pocket will benefit from the addition.

STRAIGHT ARROW

▶

The extremely narrow cedar tree (*Xanthocyparis nootkatensis* 'Green Arrow') rises like an exclamation point among the surrounding plantings in a Bremerton, Washington, garden. Golden larch (*Pseudolarix amabilis*) and red Japanese maple (*Acer palmatum*) grow just behind it, with *Magnolia sieboldii* showing its orange fall color at right and red-tipped heavenly bamboo (*Nandina domestica* 'Umpqua Warrior') in front. DESIGN John Albers, Albers Vista Gardens

THE INTERMEDIARY

◀

A tall, dense, blue Italian cypress (*Cupressus sempervirens* 'Glauca') bridges the height gap between the low border in front and the much taller Douglas firs and Western hemlocks behind in Medina, Washington. The rounded *Buxus sempervirens* 'Aureovariegata' at its left also adds heft to the border, which includes pink-flowered *Sempervivum* and variegated *Yucca filamentosa* 'Bright Edge'. The pale yellow flowers of *Scabiosa columbaria ochroleuca* 'Moon Dance' weave through the yucca. Potted red geraniums and blue *Hydrangea* 'Twist and Shout' are flanked by *Euphorbia characias wulfenii* on the left and honey bush (*Melianthus major* 'Antonow's Blue') on the right. DESIGN Daniel Mount

ILLUSION OF MOTION

◀

The upright stems of Myers asparagus fern (*A. densiflorus* 'Myers') reach across, around, and over its companions like the busy tentacles of an octopus. Without the energy of this rambunctious plant, the plain green aeonium (*A. urbicum*) and the compact shrub, *Pittosporum crassifolium* 'Nana', in this Newport Beach, California, border might look a little stiff.

CENTER STAGE

Creating vignettes—small scenes within gardens that encourage you to pause and appreciate them—is one of the greatest satisfactions in designing a garden. Concentrate these living pictures near entries, outside windows, or beside patios.

FALL SUPERSTARS

It is harder to rely on flower power for fall color in the garden than it is in spring, when hundreds of choices fill nursery shelves. Fortunately, asters light up the garden reliably from late summer well into the fall. Their nectar attracts bees and butterflies, and their daisylike blooms come in shades of lavender, blue, purple, pink, red, and white. The best of all asters is the useful and widely adapted *A.* x *frikartii*, a cross between *A. amelius* and a Himalayan species (pictured here is 'Mönch'). Forming loose mounds 2 feet tall and wide, it blooms nearly all year in mild climates if you keep spent blooms clipped off. Try it in a border behind clusters of blue fescue *(Festuca)* or black mondo grass *(Ophiopogon planiscapus)*. Or plant it beside *Rudbeckia fulgida*, whose yellow daisy flowers echo the aster's golden centers.

TRIO OF TEXTURES
◄

Glowing autumn moor grass *(Sesleria autumnalis)*, green *Sedum* 'Autumn Joy', and a shaggy-barked tree—*Melaleuca quinquenervia*—create this pocket of interest near the front door of a San Luis Obispo, California, home. DESIGN Ryan Fortini

SEASONAL FOUNTAIN
▲

A single clump of blue oat grass *(Helictotrichon sempervirens)*, carefully placed, looks as cooling as a fountain in a Northern California garden. Clumps of blooming chives *(Allium schoenoprasum)*, grown here as ornamentals, add pops of rosy purple nearby.

STAGE SET
▲

An exuberant collection of plants surrounding a tipped urn and scattered boulders suggests a slice of ancient Rome in a Woodside, California, garden. Blue lyme grass *(Leymus arenarius)*, rosy-flowered lantana, bronze *Carex*, and French lavender grow in front, while orange-flowered lion's tail *(Leonotis leonurus)* adds vivid color behind. Bronze and green phormiums behind the taller jug complete the tall backdrop. A sandy mulch finishes the vignette.

RETREATS

Not every part of a garden needs to be shared. There is much to be said for creating spaces you can enjoy when you're deliciously alone.

GREEN PEACE

◄

An alcove in a Bainbridge Island, Washington, garden, lightly filled with foliage plants in various shades of green, is as restful to look at as it is to stroll through. Japanese forest grass (*Hakonechloa macra* 'Aureola') forms the grassy fringe. It's punctuated here and there with Makino's holly ferns (*Polystichum makinoi*) and delicate white flowers, including a blooming masterwort (*Astrantia major* 'Alba') and Solomon's seal (*Polygonatum*), up front, which blooms earlier. DESIGN Tish Treherne

SOFT SCULPTURE

◄

A single Chinese elm (*Ulmus parvifolia* 'Hokkaido') rises behind a weathered log, adding a contemplative touch beside a glass fountain in a Hillsboro, Oregon, garden. Careful pruning—doable for the one-of-a-kind plant— keeps the tree shapely and gives it the look of a big bonsai.

DESIGN Laura Crockett

EVERGREEN WALLS

▲

A hedge of fern pine (*Podo-carpus gracilior*) screens al fresco showering in an Avila Beach, California, garden. Purple smoke tree (*Cotinus coggygria*), blue *Senecio mandraliscae*, and banana-leafed giant bird of paradise (*Strelitzia nicolai*) fill the small border in front.

DESIGN Ryan Fortini

⸗ *Design Element* ⸗
COLOR

Having lots of colors to consider when you design a garden is thrilling. But which ones to choose?

Start with your home. Its color, materials, and architecture will automatically narrow your choices. If you live in an ocher-tinted Mediterranean stucco, you'll want something more robust than pastels.

Now consider your style. Are you happiest in calm surroundings? Then stick to cool colors like blue and lavender. Maybe, instead, you're after drama. Then opt for hotter colors such as red or orange, which demand attention.

Remember that foliage—whether green or gray (depending on where you live)—will most likely carry the show for at least part of the year. Add a splash of burgundy foliage for visual depth, or lime-green foliage to brighten dark spaces, and you're set.

RAINBOW BLOOMS

Dahlias in vibrant hues dress the fields at Swan Island Dahlias in Canby, Oregon, with ribbons of bloom. Among the easiest perennials you can grow, the plants range from 1 to 6 feet tall and send up summer flowers in many different shapes and sizes, depending on variety. Cluster a few in borders for a bright pop of warm-season color.

⪦ Design Element ⪧
COLOR SCHEMES

MONOCHROMES

These are the easiest to design and the easiest to live with because they're inherently calming. Yellow-green to blue-green, for instance, or buttercream, daffodil, lemon, and goldenrod. If things get too serene, you can pop in a closely related hue—a dash of blue with the greens, or a bit of peach with those yellows.

❶ Chartreuse feverfew, blue-green lamb's ears, and deep green rosemary.

PAIRINGS

If shades of one color seem too tame, combine two colors for pleasing but powerful contrast. Add a few splashes of a third color, if you like, to enhance them—chartreuse with blue and yellow, or with burgundy and green.

❷ Citrus yellow Lady Bank's rose with blue-flowered *Ceanothus griseus horizontalis* 'Yankee Point'.

BRIGHTENERS

Chartreuse and lime green foliage brightens somber colors like deep green or purple and provides a lively background for marine blue flowers—especially in shade.

❸ *Salvia officinalis* 'Tricolor' (foreground), grassy *Imperata cylindrica* 'Rubra', and deep plum Japanese barberry (*Berberis thunbergii atropurpurea* 'Helmond Pillar').

SPARKLERS

White keeps pastels from fading into oblivion and prevents jewel tones from losing their richness in the sun's glare. In the shade or at twilight, it supplies welcome illumination and adds sparkle to greens.

❹ White daisies of German chamomile (*Matricaria recutita*) and golden *Coreopsis grandiflora*.

DIPLOMATS

Gray and silver are a color gardener's best friends. They mellow the heat of orange, red, and yellow and visually separate flower colors that would clash if planted beside one another, such as orange and magenta.

❺ Aloe with silver puya (*P. coerulea*).

COOLERS

Whether soft sky blue or a deep royal shade, blues complement yellow, enhance lavender, and cool the heat of orange and red. Blue blends well with most colors.

❻ Blue-flowered catmint (*Nepeta*) with orange *Kniphofia* 'Bee's Sunset'.

NEON

Brilliant scarlet, vivid orange, and hot pink are dazzling in sunlight. But because they make such strong statements, use them singly, or temper them with white-, silver-, or green-foliaged plants.

❼ *Bougainvillea* 'Barbara Karst'.

EARTH TONES

Green, straw, gold, and amber are especially effective in gardens on grassy hillsides, near the seashore, in woodlands, and in naturalistic gardens that border wildland.

❽ Amber-hued autumn fern (*Dryopteris erythrosora*) with bear's breech (*Acanthus mollis* 'Hollard's Gold').

PLUM
PERFECT

Plum, burgundy, and dark bronze
foliage plants are the horticultural
equivalent of the little black dress.
You can always count on them to look
sophisticated. One or two plants
might be enough to create the desired
effect, but, for more drama, consider
including trees or large shrubs.

POPS OF PLUM

Bronze *Carex secta* edges this Beaverton, Oregon,
garden and makes the silvery hues of *Artemisia* and
light green foliage of *Sedum* 'Autumn Joy' behind it
sparkle. Note that C. *secta* starts green and changes
color in fall; if you want an ever-brown *Carex*, try
C. *buchananii,* C. *flagellifera,* or C. *testacea.*

STELLAR SUPPORT

The green plants in this Beaverton, Oregon, garden—
from the Japanese maple (*Acer palmatum*) at left
and weeping Norway spruce (*Picea abies* 'Pendula') in center front to the distant green shrubs—
all look twice as bright thanks to their chocolate-
hued companions. Low-growing, burgundy-hued
Japanese maples grow between them. The large
dark tree at left is *Prunus cerasifera* 'Thunder-
cloud'; A. *palmatum* 'Burgundy Lace' is at right.

ELEGANTLY UPRIGHT

A vertical habit makes purple-leafed Japanese
barberry (*Berberis thunbergii atropurpurea* 'Helmond Pillar') an excellent back-of-the-border plant.
Its companions in this Seattle border are Japanese
blood grass (*Imperata cylindrica* 'Rubra') and
Oxalis corniculata. The tree is false cypress
(*Chamaecyparis obtusa* 'Gracilis').

EVER
GREEN

All-green gardens may not be the first to catch your eye, but the longer you garden, the more you appreciate them. They always look classic and inherently peaceful. Just mix them for contrasting leaf shapes and sizes, and you'll keep them interesting.

SHADE SPARKLER

◀

Unlike most *Ceanothus, C. griseus horizontalis* 'Diamond Heights' prefers some shade, even along the coast, and its bright yellow-green leaves light up those situations. Here it peeks out from beneath *Mahonia* 'Soft Caress', named for its lack of prickles, in a Menlo Park, California, garden.

TOUGH BEAUTY

▶

Despite its show-off colors, *Coprosma repens* 'Pink Splendor', left, is no diva. It tolerates most soils, coastal winds, and salt spray. Its solid green companion in this Long Beach, California, garden is tufted hair grass *(Deschampsia cespitosa* 'Schottland').

CLEVER PAIRING

▶

Black mondo grass *(Ophiopogon planiscapus* 'Nigrescens') appears to creep, spiderlike, from between upright stalks of horsetail *(Equisetum hyemale)* in a Los Gatos, California, garden, where it echoes the black rings around the horsetails' joints. Horsetail is a tough plant, but since it can be invasive, keep it confined as shown here.
DESIGN Jarrod Baumann

STEADY PRESENCE

▶

The big, frosty blue leaves of *Hosta* 'Krossa Regal' keep their hues through summer, while golden fullmoon maple *(Acer shirasawanum* 'Aureum') is a chameleon, starting the season with lemon yellow leaves, maturing to chartreuse, then becoming orange or red in fall. Both plants prefer partial shade.

FOLIAGE MASTERY

One of the advantages of designing a garden based primarily on foliage is that you can disregard color theory altogether. Warm with cool, sharp contrasts, or mellow monochromatics—all seem to work.

AMBER AND LIME
▶

A gold-leafed version of bear's breech (*Acanthus mollis* 'Hollard's Gold') warms up a Portland shade garden, along with a bronzy autumn fern (*Dryopteris erythrosora*), *Heuchera* 'Peach Flambé', and the lime-green groundcover spikemoss (*Selaginella kraussiana* 'Aurea').

SOFT CONTRAST
◀

The pale green foliage of Himalayan cedar (*Cedrus deodara* 'Silver Mist') looks twice as snow-frosted next to the deep purple of *Pennisetum advena* 'Rubrum'. Rosy-pink coneflowers (*Echinacea*) add to the show in this Portland garden.

BLUE AND PEACH
▶

The cool blue-green leaves of *Hosta* 'Halcyon' complement the warm red-orange of *Heuchera* 'Peach Flambé' in this Portland garden and will be just as compatible when the *Heuchera* foliage turns plum-purple in cold weather. Spikemoss (*Selaginella kraussiana* 'Aurea') adds a tiny splash of lime at left.

BRIGHT SPOT
▶

Three warm foliage colors and textures converge in a Northwest garden. The yellow-green at left is Japanese forest grass (*Hakonechloa macra* 'Aureola'); the small, light green conifer at right, Japanese cedar (*Cryptomeria japonica* 'Little Diamond'); and the reddish brown tangle below, dwarf rock lily (*Arthropodium candidum* 'Maculatum').

CLASSIC COMBINATION

Blue and yellow are the colors of the sea and sun. Maybe that's why they always look good together, why painters and designers favor them, and why these hues turn up together so frequently in the homes and gardens of southern France. It's a combination that never goes wrong.

PERENNIAL PARTNERS

◄

The burnished gold of yarrow (*Achillea millefolium*) and the lavender-blue of Russian sage (*Perovskia atriplicifolia*) were made for each other. The fine textures of both leaves blend together as beautifully as the colors.

ALTERNATING WAVES

◄

Bold bands of blue catmint (*Nepeta x faassenii*) and yellow yarrow (*Achillea* 'Moonshine') take turns sweeping across this Santa Fe garden. Behind them, 'Stella de Oro' daylilies and *Rosa* 'Nearly Wild' join in. DESIGN Faith Okuma

SUBTLE DRAMA

►

Flowers of bigleaf hydrangea (*H. macrophylla* 'Nigra') are so huge and the weeping form of the Japanese forest grass (*Hakonechloa macra* 'Aureola') so striking that this combination is visually powerful for lightly shaded locations.

TAMED RED

Pure red doesn't play well with other hues. It insists on standing out. The best companion for this scene stealer: neutral greens, white, or silver. Or simply combine shades of red to coral, scarlet, or pink, creating the effect of watercolors that have run together. Either way, choose reds that lean toward blue or orange; they're easier to work with in the garden.

LAVA FLOW
▶

Colors start warm, then get hotter as they spill down the slope of this Escondido, California, garden. The yellow and orange are *Leucospermum cordifolium*, a protea relative; the hot pink, bougainvillea. *Leucospermum* aren't for everyone. They are frost-sensitive, especially as young plants, and they need perfect drainage and good air circulation, making a hillside location ideal. The reward, though, is cut flowers that last up to a month in water and shrubs that, in mild winter areas, bloom half of the year.

GOES WITH EVERYTHING
▶

Burgundy-red yarrow (*Achillea millefolium* 'Summer Wine') is vivid enough to hold its own in a narrow bed beside a patio in Jackson, Wyoming.
DESIGN Mark Hershberger

ROSE PARADE
◀

A dark rose-red yarrow (*Achillea millefolium* 'Red Velvet') begins a procession of muted reds in this Dayton, Oregon, garden. Rose-pink *Echinacea purpurea* 'Doubledecker' grows beside it, followed by tall pink and coral *Agastache* 'Summer Breeze'. In the distance, a row of rose-plumed *Cotinus coggygria* 'Velvet Cloak', backed by a darker smoke tree (*C. c.* 'Royal Purple), continues the color theme. DESIGN Jacqueline Authier

RED, WHITE, AND BLUE

Red, white, and blue can either look great together, or like Fourth of July party decor, which most likely you don't want full-time. Your best bet: Combine white with either red or blue, but not both. Or, if you want to use all three colors, let one predominate; don't use equal amounts.

READY FOR THE FOURTH

◄

White-and-blue Rocky Mountain columbine (*Aquilegia coerulea*) cluster beside this front door in Snowmass, Colorado, spring through early summer, along with *Geranium* 'Johnson's Blue', which blooms nearly constantly spring through fall. DESIGN Richard Shaw

TRICOLORED ELEGANCE

►

Red *Crocosmia* 'Bright Eyes' catches your eye first in this Oregon garden, then the white spikes of *Veronicastum virginicum* 'Album'. In front, a subtle ruff of blue catmint (*Nepeta* x *faassenii*) edges the bed.

POOLS OF BLUE

►

Nepeta racemosa 'Walker's Low' offers a cool contrast to the white trunks of quaking aspen (*Populus tremuloides*) in a Jackson, Wyoming, garden. Gravel mulch meandering through the space like a silvery stream adds more white. DESIGN Mark Hershberger

WHITE SPARKLERS

►

The upright blooms of white coneflowers (*Echinacea purpurea* 'White Swan') light up a bed of red *Crocosmia* 'Bright Eyes' in a Salem, Oregon, garden.

QUIET
DRAMA

Pairing plants for strong color contrasts and using bold architectural plants as accents add drama to a simple planting. But you can command attention in quieter ways too. Try sprinkling in a little color in just the right spot, such as a space between green foliage plants.

FLASHES OF SUNLIGHT

▶

Blue-green wild rye *(Leymus condensatus* 'Canyon Prince') and dark bronze *Cordyline* form a quiet partnership for most of the year in this Paso Robles, California, garden. But come summer, *Kniphofia uvaria* 'Malibu Yellow' kicks things up a notch. Its blooms link your eye to the golden grass fields in the distance.
DESIGN Jeffrey Gordon Smith

FLICKERS OF FLAME

◀

The color scheme for this garden, in Battle Ground, Washington, is primarily variations of green. But the Japanese blood grass *(Imperata cylindrica* 'Rubra'), with its fire red tips, is used so abundantly that it creates quite an impact. A sprinkling of blue oat grass *(Helictotrichon sempervirens)* cools the fire just enough. Nootka cypress *(Xanthocyparis nootkatensis* 'Pendula'), with its Dr. Seuss shapes, adds its own drama.

BANDS OF GREEN

▶

Three rows of simple green plants, used en masse, complement the red siding of this Jackson, Wyoming, home. False spirea *(Sorbaria sorbifolia)* rises behind chartreuse-flowered lady's-mantle *(Alchemilla mollis)* near the house, while native grass, planted as sod, grows in the foreground.
DESIGN Mark Hershberg

ULTRA VIOLET

If you're attracted to monochromatic color schemes, consider shades of purple. Violet is a shy, receding color, so it doesn't rush out to meet you the way red does—but it is almost impossible to overdo. Indulge without fear.

PURPLE HAZE

▼

Though the individual flowers of Russian sage (*Perovskia atriplicifolia*) are small, collectively they create quite an effect, as they do in a Napa, California, garden.

HEAVEN SCENTS
▲

As well as having a sumptuous color—deep plum with a hint of smoke—the floribunda rose 'Ebb Tide' is richly scented. Its companion in this Los Gatos, California, garden is catmint (*Nepeta x faassenii*), which adds some earthiness to the garden's perfumes. Unlike most purple roses, this one won't fade in sunlight. DESIGN Jarrod Baumann

SUMMER SPECTACLE
▲

Certain grasses and lavenders create beautiful effects together. Here, *Lavandula x intermedia* 'Grosso' adds its violet-blue spikes to the pink plumes of *Pennisetum orientale* and the golden ones of *Miscanthus sinensis* 'Adagio' in a meadow garden in Bennett Valley, California. DESIGN Maile Arnold

MISTY MEADOW RUE

For an airy effect in lightly shaded beds, it's tough to beat meadow rue (*Thalictrum rochebrunianum*). The sturdy stems of this easy-to-grow perennial are flecked with leaves that resemble those of columbine; they form a delicate tracery that shows up best against a wall or surrounding green foliage. Sprays of small flowers appear in late spring or summer, adding lacy contrast between beefier plants. Try 'Lavender Mist' with blue or white hydrangeas, among ferns, or behind columbines. Plants grow 4 to 6 feet tall and do best in cooler climates.

SNOW-WHITE

White flowers are often used to separate two strong colors or to add crispness to a mix of pastels. But whites also work well alone. The combination of clean white flowers and dark, cool green leaves never fails to please, especially on warm days, or steely gray ones. Snowy white blooms, prime choices for twilight and evening gardens, give form to borders and beds long after other plants have disappeared.

WHITE CLOUD
◄

Most of the year, evergreen candy-tuft (*Iberis sempervirens*) is a short, neat, tough, but well-behaved mound of shiny green leaves. But in early spring, it explodes into a canopy of snowy white blooms. Its companions in this McMinnville, Oregon, garden are dwarf English boxwood (*Buxus sempervirens* 'Suffruticosa') and green lace-leaf Japanese maple (*Acer palmatum* 'Dissectum Viridis').

SUN WORSHIPPERS
▲

Santa Barbara daisy (*Erigeron karvinskianus*) looks dainty and 'Canyon Snow' Pacific Coast iris delicate, but both plants, paired here in an Orinda, California, garden, prefer full sun, not shade. These little daisies are drought-tolerant, but they do spread. Pull up young plants where you don't want them.
DESIGN Katherine Greenberg

EASIER THAN THEY LOOK

Oriental lilies look like hothouse flowers that need lots of fussing to grow, let alone bloom. But the truth is, they are among the easiest perennials you can plant. In early spring (after frost), tuck a cluster of bulbs, pointy ends up, into the ground toward the back of a border, in holes 8 inches deep and 6 inches apart. Add stakes at planting time. In mid-summer, enjoy the richly fragrant blooms ('Casa Blanca' is pictured), which unfurl in clusters atop the 3-to-5-foot stalks. Plants bloom best with regular water in summer, but need only occasional irrigation the rest of the year. And unlike other bulbs, these keep on growing even after the tops die back.

PASTELS

A garden filled with pastel flowers will always be pleasant, but it can also look a bit bland. To stir things up a bit, include a few pastels on the bright side—rose rather than pink, gold versus yellow, coral instead of peach. Then add a generous sprinkling of white or, conversely, a little splash of something dark. Plant deep blue bloom spikes beside lavender, for instance, or plum beside candy pink.

MEADOW MORNING
◄

The white flower clusters of common yarrow (*Achillea millefolium*) popping up in the midst of a sea of flax (*Linum*), past bloom and setting seed, make this Wenatchee, Washington, garden look like a meadow basking in the morning light. A few cheerful stems of yellow *Gaillardia* x *grandiflora* add more sunshine.

PURPLE PUNCH
◄

Most of the color in this border in a Bremerton, Washington, garden is pastel, starting with a silvery mound of heather (*Calluna vulgaris* 'Silver Knight'). But a large patch of yellow *Achillea* 'Moonshine' and the pale pink and brighter pink of tree mallows (*Lavatera* x *clementii* 'Barnsley') add punch, while rich blue-violet English lavender (*Lavandula angustifolia*), center, jolts everything awake. DESIGN John Albers, Albers Vista Gardens

WHITE RIBBON
►

A winding river of Shasta daisies (*Leucanthemum* x *superbum* 'Alaska') brightens up a border of purple coneflowers (*Echinacea purpurea* 'Prairie Splendor') and gold *Achillea* 'Moonshine' in Jackson, Wyoming.

BURGUNDY AND CHARTREUSE

Burgundy and chartreuse can look stunning together. The key to keeping this combo from looking too intense: Tone it down by including other foliage colors. Blue-greens and bronzes are particularly effective.

GOLDEN DRIFTS

▶

Pfitzer juniper (*Juniperus x pfitzeriana* 'Aurea Improved') and a burgundy-leafed coral bell (*Heuchera* 'Crimson Curls') create a striking combo that complements the hues of the building behind.

SUBTLE MIX

◀

Burgundy and chartreuse are the most striking colors in this border at the Bellevue Botanical Garden, Washington. The former is supplied by two forms of *Berberis;* the latter by the chartreuse flowers of lady's-mantle (*Alchemilla mollis*). Other foliage colors and the brown seed heads of ornamental onion (*Allium*) soften the contrast.

STAR POWER

▶

Euphorbia characias wulfenii is a nearly flawless plant, with showy chartreuse flowers that last forever and light up any other color beside them. The plant's blue-green foliage is also attractive. In this Whidbey Island, Washington, garden, it blooms among burgundy *Berberis thunbergii* 'Crimson Pygmy', dwarf mugo pine (*Pinus mugo mugo*), mahonia, and rugosa roses.
DESIGN Stacie Crooks

SPOTS
OF SILVER

Silvery gray and frosty blue foliage seem custom-made for warm climates. Just looking at them makes you feel cooler. The same hues work a different kind of magic in cold climates. Under overcast skies, their colors sparkle, warming things up.

COOL GLAMOUR

▲

Blue fescue (*Festuca glauca*) and silver puya (*P. coerulea x violacea*) shimmer in the sun, looking even more frosty thanks to their dark companion, *Phormium* 'Amazing Red'. The fourth plant is thread-leaf nandina (*N. domestica* 'Filamentosa'). The brushed stainless steel wall screen behind the plants (disguising a concrete block wall) contributes additional glamour in this Los Gatos, California, garden. DESIGN Jarrod Baumann

SILVER SPLASH

◄

A soft, mounding *Juniperus virginiana* 'Grey Owl' adds gentle contrast beside apple green grasses in this free-form border. It grows slowly to 3 feet tall and 6 feet wide, and needs only occasional water once established. Give it full sun (part shade in the desert).

BOLD STYLE

▲

Mexican tree ocotillos (*Fouquieria macdougalii*) spread elegant fans behind equally spaced agaves (A. 'Blue Glow') in this California garden, where they complement a contemporary-style home. Feathery chartreuse *Sedum rupestre* 'Angelina' covers the ground between them. Fruitless, silvery-foliaged olive trees (*Olea europaea* 'Bonita') add soft textures nearby.
DESIGN Daniel Nolan

⸗ *Design Element* ⸗
LAYERS

Plunk a few varieties of shrubs and perennials into the ground in a straight line, and you'll end up with a boring, one-dimensional border. But if you want a seamless tapestry effect, layering the plants by height—shortest in front to tallest in back—is essential. So is giving each plant the space it needs to develop its natural shape, offsetting each plant slightly from its neighbors, and letting all the plants grow and mingle together.

Start in the back. If you have room, plant some trees, vines, or medium to tall shrubs for screening. For the middle of the border, select a range of shrubs—tall ones as well as more compact ones. Fill in with perennials and ornamental grasses of varying heights. Finally, plant groundcovers in front to knit everything together.

But in quiet times between blooms, the rich intricacy of the layering holds its own.

CLOUDS OF FOLIAGE

A pink pincushion (*Leucospermum*) and two kinds of *Leucadendron* create successive layers of interest in a Northern California garden. These South African natives are fairly drought-tolerant, but they do demand full sun and soil with perfect drainage, such as on gentle slopes.

SLOPES

When planting slopes, there is more to think about than just holding the soil in place—though that is always the first consideration. You also need to select the mix of plant sizes, shapes, and colors you'll see vertically. Do you want a beautiful view as an extension of your garden? Or do you need something more pedestrian such as a way to obscure the driveway? Plant accordingly.

ARTFUL TRANSITION

▶

Ornamental grasses—dark green *Festuca californica* and blue *Helictotrichon sempervirens*—grow at the top of this slope in Walnut Creek, California, where they visually connect the garden to the protected open space beyond. Farther downslope toward the patio, the plantings are greener and more floriferous, with 'Goodwin Creek Grey' lavender, 'Garnet' penstemon, prostrate rosemary, and Santa Barbara daisy (*Erigeron karvinskianus*) providing pops of flower color. DESIGN Stephan Thuilot

SIMULATED SLOPE

▶

This Tucson border is perfectly flat. But trailing lantana, planted behind the large boulders and encouraged to spill out between them, creates the illusion of a slight slope. Both of these lantana varieties—'New Gold' and 'Monine'—are guaranteed trailers. *Yucca rostrata* 'Sapphire Skies' fans out its foliage from behind the boulder.

TROPICAL PASSAGE

◀

Tasmanian tree ferns (*Dicksonia antarctica*) flanking the stone steps give this Avila Beach, California, garden the look of a tropical resort. The rest of the plants are more drought-tolerant than the ferns. They include purple smoke tree (*Cotinus coggygria*) and *Aeonium arboreum*; the blue-greens of *Euphorbia characias wulfenii* 'Shorty' and torch lily (*Kniphofia uvaria*); and the pure greens of *Agave attenuata* and autumn moor grass (*Sesleria autumnalis*). Feathery papyrus (*Cyperus papyrus*) grows at the top of the stairs. DESIGN Ryan Fortini

GROUND HUGGERS

Where there's a view to preserve, whether of a lake, forest, or distant mountain—or simply pretty views of the garden's far corners—you can layer on the low plantings to create interest.

PRIMARY COLORS
▶

Mounding perennials fill a planting strip in Santa Fe, giving the long, narrow space energy and interest. They include, front to back, catmint (*Nepeta* x *faassenii* 'Select Blue'), red Jupiter's beard (*Centranthus ruber*), silvery 'Powis Castle' artemisia, deep blue 'May Night' salvia, sunny 'Sterntaler' coreopsis, more Jupiter's beard, and yellow 'Moonshine' yarrow. DESIGN Julia Berman

TAPESTRY EFFECT
◀

Heath, in various colors, weaves a patterned living rug in this Whidbey Island, Washington, garden, staying low enough to frame but not block the garden's enviable view. The heaths include *Erica* x *darleyensis* 'Mediterranean White' and red *Calluna vulgaris* 'Firefly'. The rest, all with pink blooms, are 'Mediterranean Pink' (pale), 'Furzey' (medium), 'J.W. Porter' (dark), and 'Kramer's Rote' (very dark). *Spiraea japonica* 'Goldmound', up front, and a row of chartreuse-flowered *Euphorbia characias wulfenii* spice up the pastels. DESIGN Stacie Crooks

TEXTURAL TWIST
◀

Golden prickly pear cactus (*Opuntia aurea*) adds heft to fine-stemmed, small-leafed flowering perennials in this Colorado border. They include *Agastache* 'Acapulco', with tall spikes of pink blooms; *Salvia microphylla* 'Hot Lips', whose white and red blooms create a spatter-paint effect at left; and, up front, rose-pink Jupiter's beard (*Centranthus ruber*). DESIGN Kelly Grummons

THE LATE SHOW

Toward summer's end, just when most flowering plants are starting to appear a little bit tired, smoke trees *(Cotinus coggygria)* can look their most glorious. That's when dramatic puffs of "smoke" from tiny withering flowers appear on the branches. In the Dayton, Oregon, garden pictured above, they steal the show from lower growing plants in front—even a *Sedum* 'Autumn Joy' barely visible below it. For desert gardens, Apache plume *(Fallugia paradoxa)* is similar, but sports paler pink clouds. Still prefer flowers for late-season drama? Try Copper Canyon daisy *(Tagetes lemmonii)* or a perennial sunflower *(Helianthus)* such as *H. maximilianii* or *H.* 'Lemon Queen'. DESIGN Jacqueline Authier

MOUNDS

Shrubs and perennials are garden mainstays, used most often in borders and foundation plantings. But they can play other roles as well. Widely space them to create islands of texture and color among low meadow grasses, or use them as soft green backdrops for more dramatic plants.

SOFT BACKDROP

◄

Upright rosemary forms a silvery green curtain behind purple-tinged *Sedum telephium* 'Matrona' in a Dayton, Oregon, garden.

SUPPORT CAST

▶

Cool blue *Senecio mandraliscae* (foreground), along with green and yellow rosettes of *Aeonium* 'Kiwi' in front of a spray of variegated *Furcraea foetida mediopicta*, complement the once-in-a-lifetime bloom spikes of a pair of agaves (*A. desmettiana* 'Variegata') in a Mission Hills, California, garden. DESIGN Randy Laurie

SANTA FE SPLENDOR

◄

Rabbitbrush (*Chrysothamnus nauseosus*) adds sunbursts of fluffy yellow flowers in this Santa Fe meadow garden, putting on a dazzling show beside sunflowers in late summer. A big blue cloud of Russian sage (*Perovskia atriplicifolia*) cools things down just enough.

SPLASHES

▼

Japanese tassel fern (*Polystichum polyblepharum*) holds its fronds above a low-growing *Epimedium* and a few delicate sprays of white-flowered sweet woodruff (*Galium odoratum*) in the front of a Medina, Washington, border. The whitewashed leaves and tiny blue flowers of *Brunnera macrophylla* 'Jack Frost' fleck the next row. Japanese maple in back adds another wave of green. DESIGN Daniel Mount and Gavin Martin

DRIFTS

Broad bands of similar or identical plants that weave themselves together seamlessly can create striking tapestry effects in borders. To achieve this effortless look, combine different plants of the same height and color in each "wave," whether shades of green or pairs of pinks. Or mass single species of heather, say, in waves by color as pictured above right.

RIPPLES

▲

Heath (*Erica*) and heather provide abundant winter color in this Whidbey Island, Washington, border. *Erica x darleyensis* 'Mediterranean White' connects the various waves, with magenta *E.* 'Kramer's Rote' appearing to flow inward from the sides, and red *Calluna vulgaris* 'Firefly' tucked up front. In back, dormant bloodtwig dogwoods (*Cornus sanguinea* 'Midwinter Fire') mingle with dwarf mugo pine (*Pinus mugo mugo*). Heathers and heaths need fast-draining soil. DESIGN Stacie Crooks

FROTH

◄

Purple coneflowers (*Echinacea purpurea* 'Merlot') and a large swath of knotweed (*Persicaria amplexicaulis* 'Firetail') make up this long rosy ribbon in a Corbett, Oregon, garden. A mass planting of blue-flowered *Geranium* 'Rozanne' weaves through both. DESIGN Darcy Daniels

TORCH SONG

▲

A generous clump of orange torch lily (*Kniphofia* 'Shining Scepter') adds punch to cool greens in a Silverton, Oregon, garden. The white-striped grass is *Miscanthus sinensis* 'Cabaret'.

SUNSET HUES

◀

Coral has a strong presence, especially if used abundantly and combined with light-colored foliage plants. In this Los Gatos, California, garden, *Leucadendron* 'Jester', whose variegated leaves are tinged with coral, echoes the coral flowers of *Aloe striata* behind. The big, sunny face of *Aeonium* 'Sunburst' and a blond mane of a feather grass add further warmth. DESIGN Jarrod Baumann

DESERT GLOW

▶

Native palo verde trees (*Parkinsonia*) light up gardens all over the desert in early spring. In this Southwest garden, *P.* 'Desert Museum', with golden yellow flowers, creates a glowing backdrop for a low border in front. It contains pink Mexican evening primrose (*Oenothera speciosa*); golden barrel cactus (*Echinocactus grusonii*); white-flowered blackfoot daisy (*Melampodium leucanthum*); yellow-flowered Indian mallow (*Abutilon palmeri*); and *Salvia greggii* 'Furman's Red'. DESIGN Faith Okuma

SHOCK WAVES

Every garden needs a pop of orange—if you're brave—or yellow, to brighten things up. No other colors warm up the garden quite like these. Jolts of orange hold their own in glaring sun, while yellows lighten up even shady corners.

GOLD
RUSH

A single yellow-flowered plant can light up a whole garden. Flannel bush (*Fremontodendron*) is a radiant example; it covers itself with golden blooms in spring. Not every garden has room for this big California native. It can reach 20 feet tall and 12 feet wide. In smaller spaces, try Indian mallow (*Abutilon palmeri*), another unthirsty, yellow-flowered native shrub, which grows 3 to 5 feet tall and as wide. Among non-natives, lantana is a nearly indestructible shrub, available in many shades of yellow. Among easy-care perennials with golden blooms, try black-eyed Susan (*Rudbeckia hirta*), sundrops (*Calylophus hartwegii*), *Gazania* hybrids, and 'Bush Gold' kangaroo paw (*Anigozanthos*).

DELICIOUS MIXES

Foliage may not be the first thing you notice in a pretty garden, but foliage plants are border essentials. They provide richly varied leaf textures that keep monochromatic gardens from looking dull, or they add contrasting colors that either enliven quiet greens or mellow the heat of two strong companions.

ARTIST'S HUES

▶

Reds, yellows, and blues—the primary colors used by artists—accent this border in a Seattle garden. Jerusalem sage (Phlomis fruticosa) provides a big punch of mellow yellow in the center, while Japanese barberry (Berberis thunbergii atropurpurea 'Crimson Pgymy'), the shrub up front on the far right, provides the red. A true geranium (G. himalayense 'Gravetye'), in the center front, with bluish purple flowers, and a Ceanothus thyrsiflorus 'Victoria', toward the back, provide the blue. A small, silvery blue Eucalyptus gunnii grows in front of the ceanothus. The green mounds edging the border include Erica x darleyensis 'Mary Helen', in front, and a Bergenia 'Bressingham Ruby', to its right. DESIGN Stacie Crooks

RASPBERRY SWIRL

◀

A generous drift of pink Scotch heather (Calluna vulgaris 'Firefly') in the front of this Seattle border appears to ramble toward an upright deep burgundy Berberis thunbergii 'Helmond Pillar' and a taller Japanese maple Acer palmatum 'Bloodgood', behind. Various green-foliaged plants surround this ribbon of raspberry. They include a box-leafed honeysuckle (Lonicera pileata) just to the right of the heather; Cryptomeria japonica 'Sekkan-sugi' immediately behind the heather, with bronze-tinged vine maple (Acer circinatum) to its left; and dark green Austrian pine (Pinus nigra) at the very back. The gray leaves of bush daisy (Brachyglottis 'Sunshine'), to the right of the Berberis, add some sparkle. DESIGN Stacie Crooks

HOT SPOTS

▶

Winged euonymus (E. alatus), dressed in its summer-green leaves, is a cooling mediator between a golden-leafed Spiraea japonica 'Goldflame', in the foreground, and a deep burgundy Japanese barberry (Berberis thunbergii atropurpurea). In fall, after the spirea's pink flowers have disappeared, the euonymus leaves turn fiery red-orange, creating a different but equally dramatic picture.

Design Element
SEASONS

There is something deeply satisfying about a garden that changes with the calendar: spring blooms, summer grasses, fall leaves, and winter berries making their appearance, one after another, like a succession of gifts, reminding you to enjoy the season while it's there. This magic requires a little advance planning.

To start the show, plant bulbs that naturalize easily in your area. Indulge in your favorite spring-flowering shrubs and perennials for high season, but leave room for things that come into their own in late summer—asters, goldenrod, salvias such as 'Indigo Spires', and tawny ornamental grasses.

To light up the fall, add a deciduous tree whose leaves color spectacularly, such as Japanese maple.

A layered garden provides fresh attractions throughout the year.

128

BLAZING LEAVES

A Japanese maple
(*Acer palmatum*)
spreads a cloud
of glowing orange
foliage over a
Portland garden.

FOUR SEASONS OF COLOR

For beds and borders that look striking in every season, include clusters of easy-care bulbs and perennials for bloom in spring and summer, shrubs or small trees whose foliage turns vibrant orange, plum, or golden yellow in fall. In snow country, leave seed heads on grasses to give shape to border edgings.

❶ SPRING

For bursts of spring bloom, tuck a cluster of bulbs among lower growing shrubs. Here, spikes of golden foxtail lily (*Eremurus robustus*) and smaller spikes of maiden's wreath (*Francoa ramosa*) tower above golden *Spiraea japonica* 'Magic Carpet' in a Seattle garden. Behind them, *Geranium psilostemon* chimes in with magenta blooms. A dark purple *Clematis* 'Jackmanii' grows in back.
DESIGN Stacie Crooks

② SUMMER

The sunny upturned faces of black-eyed Susan (*Rudbeckia hirta*) match the spirit of summer perfectly. Here they are joined by purple coneflower (*Echinacea purpurea*) and purple prairie clover (*Dalea purpurea*), creating the effect of a prairie in full bloom.

③ FALL

Coral bark maple (*Acer palmatum* 'Sango Kaku'), the orange-leafed tree to the right, is the obvious star in this Portland garden in autumn. But the red-leafed *Loropetalum chinense* 'Pipa's Red' under the tree also contributes flaming hues. A low, bluish cedar just left of the path provides a steady presence. Grasses—*Miscanthus sinensis* 'Morning Light' toward the back and low *Carex albula* 'Frosty Curls' up front—create movement. DESIGN Darcy Daniels

④ WINTER

The upright seed heads of feather reed grass (*Calamagrostis* x *acutiflora* 'Karl Foerster') ride high above the foliage, adding interest to a narrow bed in Denver. Snow that collects on the foliage gives form to the planting.

EARLY SUMMER

◄

Foliage is lush and flowers plentiful in this Portland garden. The chokeberry (Aronia) left of the path is covered with milky white blooms, while a yellow Japanese forest grass (Hakonechloa macra 'Areola') spills out onto the path beyond. On the right side of the path, two types of moor grass are blooming—Molinia caerulea 'Variegata', up front, and taller M. c. arundinacea 'Skyracer', near the gate, flank blue-flowered true geranium and a Sedum 'Autumn Joy' getting ready to flower. Variegated dogwood (Cornus alba 'Elegantissima') beyond the gate is cloaked in yellow-green leaves. DESIGN Darcy Daniels

FALL

◄

In this same Portland garden, grasses carry the show along the same path; though dormant, they still create interest. The moor grasses (Molina caerulea) have turned amber-gold; the Japanese forest grass (Hakonechloa macra) is a darker shade of brown. Behind the gate, the dogwood (Cornus alba) has dropped its leaves, revealing its handsome branch structure.

FALL STARS

►

Evergreens predominate most of the year in this Bremerton, Washington, garden. But in fall, a burgundy-leafed dogwood (Cornus alba 'Kesselingii') is backed by bursts of golden foliage on 'Autumn Moon' maple (Acer shirasawanum), left, and another dogwood (C. alba 'Bud's Yellow'), right. A swath of heather (Calluna vulgaris) up front contributes a second broad stroke of red. The blue-gray foliage of white rockrose (Cistus x hybridus) and woolly thyme (Thymus serpyllum) adds a few cool splashes. DESIGN John Albers, Albers Vista Gardens

TUCK IN SOME GARDEN ART

Even the sleepiest border can come alive in fall and winter with the right piece of garden art. In this Portland garden, a pair of oversize flower sculptures add a bold accent to soft, bright chartreuse leaves of Japanese forest grass (Hakonechloa macra 'All Gold'). DESIGN Mike Darcy

SEASONAL FOLIAGE

Gardens are always at their most glorious in early summer. But you want them to look good in the quieter seasons too—especially in cold climates where deciduous plants go dormant for winter. To do that, include ornamental grasses—they're showy, even when dormant. Just leave their seed heads in place over winter to capture frost and snow.

ONE PLANT—
THREE SEASONS

Some plants are chameleons. They change every season. One of these champions might be all you need to keep your garden attractive year-round. Two or more can make the greenest summer garden look entirely different in fall.

SUMMER
▼

Redtwig dogwood (*Cornus sericea*), growing under aspen and cottonwood trees on either side of an irrigation channel in Snowmass, Colorado, barely gets your attention. The freshness of new grass and tree foliage are the season's highlights.
DESIGN Richard Shaw

FALL
▲

The redtwig dogwood has grown taller and sports red foliage and the red twigs and branches it was named for, creating a beautiful contrast with the blonds of grasses and gold aspen leaves.

WINTER

◄

The dogwood has dropped its leaves to expose red stems, which add a jolt of bright color to the bare, snowy white winter garden. Only the new branches and twigs of this dogwood are intense red, though, so cut back these shrubs severely late in the dormant season to get the same results the following year. Bloodtwig dogwood (*Cornus sanguinea*), which has darker, near-purple stems, should be treated the same way.

PLANNING FOR TRANSITIONS

Gardens can look rather empty in early spring, especially in cool winter climates before deciduous perennials put out new growth. But if you include one or two early-blooming shrubs that will flower before new foliage appears, they'll gather all the attention so you won't notice the bare ground. This border, in a Portland front yard, offers lessons in planning for graceful transitions from season to season, thanks to its well-orchestrated mix of evergreen and deciduous plants.

SPRING

▶

Two shrubs steal the scene. Creamy yellow flowers cloak the bare branch tips on a paper bush (*Edgeworthia chrysantha*), center; the plant will put on another show at the end of the year when its leaves turn gold. The other star, at the far end of the border, *Stachyurus praecox*, drapes its catkin-like flowers on bare branches; by late summer, the flowers will have turned into yellow berries. Evergreens make up the border's all-season mainstays. They include (foreground from left) grasslike *Carex conica* 'Hime Kan Suge' and a soft, mounding hemlock (*Tsuga canadensis* 'Moon Frost'); a deep green, spreading yew (*Taxus x media* 'Densiformis'), left of the paper bush; Hinoki false cypress (*Chamaecyparis obtusa* 'Filicoides Compacta'); and compact *Cryptomeria japonica* 'Rein's Dense Jade' at the far end, which turns bronzy purple in winter. Golden Japanese forest grass (*Hakonechloa macra* 'Aureola'), center, is just leafing out. DESIGN Darcy Daniels

SUMMER

◄

The paper bush and *Stachyurus praecox* (far left in lower left photo) are fully leafed out, as are the reddish mat of *Sedum spurium* 'Dragon's Blood'; the golden Japanese forest grass, up front; and a brownish *Berberis thunbergii* 'Orange Rocket', left of the paper bush. At the border's far end (left), a reddish green, grasslike *Astelia nervosa* 'Westland'; a blue hosta (*H.* 'Halcyon'); and a golden Japanese forest grass are similarly at their lushest in summer.

TIPS *from a* PRO

Garden designer and educator **STACIE CROOKS** has created gardens throughout the Pacific Northwest, where she specializes in drought-tolerant, low-maintenance, environmentally friendly landscapes. "Flowers come and go, but structural evergreen plants look good most of the year."

LIGHT

Mix in plants whose leaves reflect light, or glow when backlit, such as viburnums and Japanese maples.

CONTRAST

Set big-leafed plants beside fine-leafed ones. Blend soft-textured plants with structural ones, spiky with rounded leaves.

COLOR

Spice up a mostly green palette with variegated plants that provide hits of gold, bronze, and purple. "Pair a viburnum with a yew, then throw in a *Sedum* 'Autumn Joy' and black-eyed Susan (*Rudbeckia fulgida* 'Goldsturm'), and you've got it all," she says.

SEASONAL
STRATEGIES

Even borders composed largely of evergreen and deciduous shrubs can benefit from a few bursts of color spring through fall, or strong, shapely evergreens in winter. Here are three ways to go.

TUCK IN BULBS OR ANNUALS

◄

Summer flowers fleck this mostly green border in a Washington garden. They include orange and yellow marigolds (*Tagetes patula* 'France's Choice'), a spray of perennial red 'Urchin' dahlias; *Amaranthus* 'Kerala Red'; and sunny perennial *Helianthus* x *multiflorus* 'Flore Pleno'. The purple leaves of smoke tree (*Cotinus coggygria* 'Velvet Cloak') and the big blue-gray ones of *Melianthus major* add permanent interest to a border between meadow grass and Western red cedar. DESIGN Daniel Mount

LAYER ON THE COLOR

▶

Knotweed (*Persicaria amplexicaulis* 'Golden Arrow'), with red bloom spikes in late summer, creates a few sparks of its own up front, while deciduous trees cloaked with fall color energize the rest of this Washington garden. They include burgundy Japanese barberry (*Berberis thunbergii atropurpurea* 'Rose Glow') and, just in front of it, seven sons flower (*Heptacodium miconioides*), and Canadian serviceberry (*Amelanchier canadensis*), the bright orange tree at the back. Atlas cedar, which has weeping branches of blue needles, grows in the center. DESIGN John Albers, Albers Vista Gardens

PLANT A CONIFER

▶

Well-chosen conifers in a Washington garden add interest when deciduous trees have dropped their leaves and nothing is in bloom. In front is the false cypress *Chamaecyparis pisifera filifera* 'Mops'; immediately behind it is the beautifully named Japanese black pine (*Pinus thunbergii* 'Thunderhead'). In the background, Japanese cedar (*Cryptomeria japonica* 'Sekkan-sugi') echoes the pine's bright shimmer. The red berries of heavenly bamboo (*Nandina domestica* 'Umpqua Warrior') add a small pop of color. DESIGN John Albers, Albers Vista Gardens

⸘ Smart Choices ⸛
SHRUBS

These are a garden's backbones. Their primary purpose is to give it structure. Colorful foliage or showy flowers are a bonus.

STAPLES

Not all plants need to be stars. You also want something quieter for backdrops, hedges, or edging.

COAST ROSEMARY (Westringia fruticosa) This dense Australian shrub has gray-green leaves and small, white or lavender flowers. Tolerates wind and drought.

PITTOSPORUM For light screening, use *P. tenuifolium* 'Silver Sheen' or 'Marjorie Channon'; for low borders, *P. t.* 'Golf Ball'; *P. tobira* 'Wheeler's Dwarf'; or *P. t.* 'Cream de Mint'.

COLORFUL FOLIAGE

These shrubs have leaves that show some color and add interest to the garden.

COMMON NINEBARK (Physocarpus opulifolius 'Coppertina') This 6-to-8-foot-tall deciduous shrub has coppery orange foliage that shows off beautifully against blond grasses. 'Lady in Red' is smaller (4 to 6 feet) with purplish red foliage.

COPROSMA Super-glossy leaves come in nearly unbelievable colors on plants that are tough as nails. Mirror plant (*C. repens* 'Pink Splendor') has green leaves with yellow margins and a pink blush. (For shorter hybrids, see pages 266–267.)

HEAVENLY BAMBOO (Nandina domestica) Leaves begin bronze-pink, then become fiery in cold weather. Creamy flowers and red berries are bonuses. 'Obsession' and 'Flirt' have deep red new growth.

'KALEIDOSCOPE' ABELIA (A. x grandiflora 'Kaleidoscope') A dwarf, easy-care, evergreen shrub. Its chameleon-like foliage changes with the seasons from golden yellow in spring to orange-red in fall.

RED-LEAF JAPANESE BARBERRY (Berberis thunbergii atropurpurea) Deciduous shrub with small leaves in red to reddish purple. 'Helmond Pillar' is columnar to 6 feet tall; 'Crimson Pygmy' grows 2 feet tall.

SMOKE TREE (Cotinus) Tall shrub often trained as a small tree; beloved for its near-purple leaves and dramatic puffs of "smoke" from fading flowers. Look for *C. coggygria* 'Royal Purple' or *C. c.* 'Velvet Cloak'.

YELLOW-LEAFED SPIREA The combo of chartreuse leaves and pink flowers sizzles. Try *Spiraea japonica* 'Goldmound', 'Goldflame', or 'Magic Carpet'.

MACHO MEDITERRANEANS

These plants are drought-tolerant—with silvery leaves.

BUSH GERMANDER (Teucrium fruticans) Silver stems and leaves with white undersides create a shimmering appearance. Small lavender-pink flowers are present much of the year.

LAVENDER English lavender (*L. angustifolia*) is best for cold climates. *L. a.* 'Munstead' and Lavandin types such as *L. x intermedia* and *L. x* 'Grosso' are the most fragrant. (For container varieties, see pages 266–267.)

ROSEMARY (Rosmarinus officinalis) Resinous, aromatic foliage; attractive dense habit. 'Irene' and 'Ken Taylor' are trailing types. 'Blue Spires' and 'Tuscan Blue' grow upright.

SANTOLINA (S. chamaecyparissus) Dense mounds of whitish gray foliage. Ideal for border edges.

SHOWY FLOWERS

These shrubs rival perennials for their flower displays.

BIRD OF PARADISE (Caesalpinia) Tropical American shrubs with ferny leaves. Bright flowers are favorites for desert gardens: *C. gilliesii*, yellow; *C. pulcherrima*, orange or red. Blooms attract hummingbirds.

BOTTLEBRUSH (Callistemon) Bristly red flowers cover plants in spring. *C. citrinus* 'Slim', tall and narrow, is great for tight spaces. *C. viminalis* 'Little John' is compact.

CALIFORNIA WILD LILAC (Ceanothus) California natives with flowers in shades of blue. Good varieties include 'Concha', 'Dark Star', and 'Julia Phelps'. *C. griseus horizontalis* 'Diamond Heights' has striking two-tone leaves. (For groundcover types, see pages 234–235.)

CAPE PLUMBAGO (P. auriculata) This mounding shrub (to 6 feet tall) is prized for its rounded clusters of sky blue flowers. It thrives in the West's warm climates, in sun or light shade, and needs little to no water once established.

FLOWERING POMEGRANATE (Punica granatum) Showy deciduous ornamentals that produce red-orange flowers with ruffled edges, often followed by decorative fruits. The plant thrives in heat and takes moderate water. Compact types include 'Nana', which grows to 3 feet tall.

HYDRANGEA Garden hydrangeas (*H. macrophylla*), with large flower clusters, are best for mild winter climates. Oakleaf types (*H. quercifolia*), such as 'Snow Queen', have long white flower clusters and leaves that turn color in fall. *H. paniculata* 'Limelight' flowers open pale green, then fade to soft pink. (For dwarf forms, see pages 266–267.)

LION'S TAIL (Leonotis leonurus) This mint-family relative sends up whorls of furry, deep orange flowers in fall.

PRIDE OF MADEIRA (Echium candicans) Towering spikes of blue-violet flowers appear in spring. The shrub is great for creating bold effects against walls or at the backs of borders. Cut off faded blooms to prevent rampant reseeding.

ROCKROSE (Cistus) In their favored dry-summer climate, these Mediterranean natives cover themselves with flowers from spring to early summer. They tolerate drought and are often planted in fire-hazard areas and on dry banks. Crimson-spot rockrose (*C. ladanifer*) has white blooms with a crimson spot at each petal base; *C. x crispatus* 'Warley Rose' has pink blooms; and orchid rockrose (*C. x purpureus*) has reddish purple blooms—it's especially showy beside *Ceanothus* 'Julia Phelps', with deep indigo blue flowers.

SALVIA Among favorites: *S.* 'Wendy's Wish', a small shrub with large, purple-red flowers growing from brown calyxes; *S. microphylla* 'Berzerkeley', with magenta-pink blooms; and *S. m.* 'Hot Lips', whose white flowers are edged in lipstick red.

1 *Cotinus* 'Grace'
2 *Caesalpinia pulcherrima*
3 *Salvia microphylla* 'Hot Lips'
4 Lion's tail (*Leonotis leonurus*)
5 English lavender (*Lavandula angustifolia*)
6 California wild lilac (*Ceanothus impressus* 'Puget Blue')
7 *Hydrangea paniculata* 'Limelight'
8 *Coprosma repens* 'Pink Splendor'

140

PERENNIALS

Perennials are synonymous with showy flowers—no argument there. But that's not their only value. Many are grown strictly for foliage.

SUMMER STANDOUTS

Summer is when flowering perennials peak. Here are some of the easiest and most satisfying plants to grow.

AGASTACHE Upright stems packed with whorls of pink, purple, blue, red, or orange flowers that attract hummingbirds, butterflies, and bees. Licorice mint (*A. rupestris*) has an especially delicious scent.

BLANKET FLOWER (Gaillardia x grandiflora) Compact bloomers with daisylike flowers in hot colors. The plant thrives in heat, blooms until frost, and, as a bonus, attracts butterflies. 'Arizona Sun', 'Goblin', 'Fanfare', 'Burgunder', and 'Tokajer' last longer than most.

CONEFLOWER (Echinacea) Daisy-like flowers with large cone-shaped centers come in many colors, from pink and orange to lime green.

PENSTEMON Tubular flowers attract butterflies and hummingbirds. Hybrids, which can handle regular watering, are more adaptable than the species. They include 'Apple Blossom', 'Garnet', and 'Midnight'. Among the easier native types are firecracker penstemon (*P. eatonii*), *P. heterophyllus* 'Margarita BOP', *P. strictus*, *P. pinifolius*, and *P. pseudospectabilis*.

RUDBECKIA A golden daisy with a long bloom season. Black-eyed Susan (*R. hirta*) comes in many splendid forms but tends to be short-lived. *R. fulgida sullivantii* 'Goldsturm' is particularly choice—it lasts longer.

SALVIA Among the best summer bloomers, in shades of blue, are *S.* 'Indigo Spires', *S.* x *sylvestris*, *S. nemorosa*, *S.* 'Purple Majesty', and *S. leucantha* 'Midnight'.

For fall bloom, it's tough to beat Mexican sage (*S. mexicana* 'Limelight'), which can reach 8 feet tall or more and sends up spikes of dark blue flowers with chartreuse bracts, and pineapple sage (*S. elegans* 'Golden Delicious'), which grows 3 feet tall with yellow-green leaves that set off spikes of fire-engine red blooms.

TRUE GERANIUM Mounding understory plants with lots of small, single flowers. Best where summers are cool and mild. Many wonderful blues, including 'Johnson's Blue' and 'Rozanne'. *G.* x *cantabrigiense* 'Biokovo', a pink-blushed white; *G.* x *oxonianum* 'Wargrave Pink'; and magenta-purple 'Ann Folkard' are also winners.

LATE BLOOMERS

There are fewer flower choices in fall than in spring or summer, but fortunately they are great ones.

ASTER Wide range of colors, but the blues are the best complement for buff grasses and goldenrod. *Aster* x *frikartii* is a stellar variety. Also try *A. novae-belgii* 'Professor Anton Kippenberg', *A. novae-angliae* 'Purple Dome', and *A. oblongifolius* 'October Skies'.

GOLDENROD (Solidago) Cheerful plumes of bright gold. Great late-season nectar source for butterflies, and birds seek out the seeds that follow. Should be grown more, but people mistakenly believe it causes hay fever; goldenrod is *not* allergenic.

SEDUM *S. spectabile* and *S. telephium* have slightly different leaves, but the two succulent perennials are otherwise similar. Both put on a long show—their flower buds look like little cabbages atop stems; the flowers open pink, then slowly mature to decorative brown seed heads. 'Autumn Joy' is the best-known variety.

MOSTLY FOLIAGE

These perennials are grown primarily for their foliage, which provides contrasting textures in a border.

ASTELIA (A. chathamica x nervosa 'Silver Shadow') Bold, strappy foliage has a striking metallic silver sheen. The plant forms a fountain effect in borders. It's best in part shade.

DUSTY MILLER (Senecio cineraria) This tough Mediterranean perennial has lacy, woolly white leaves—striking in night gardens. It takes full sun and little water, but needs soil with good drainage. Yellow flowers are a bonus.

HOSTA Queen of the shade garden, especially in cool summer areas such as the Pacific Northwest. Broad leaves in splendid solids and patterns, often crinkled, glossy, or wavy-edged. Pure blue forms, such as 'Halcyon', are top sellers. Chartreuse types, such as 'Sum and Substance', make good partners or can lighten up the shade all on their own.

JAPANESE FOREST GRASS (Hakonechloa macra) Graceful, arching grass. Gold-leafed 'Aureola' is the most widely grown variety. Perfect accent plant.

EDGERS

Like a cuff with lace, a border often looks better with a decorated edge.

BIDENS FERULIFOLIA Forms mounds or spills over a border, depending on variety. Vibrant, honey-scented, golden yellow flowers bloom almost continually in mild weather; they attract bees and butterflies.

CORAL BELLS (Heuchera) Compact, mounding, evergreen plants prized for their striking foliage colors, from caramel and lime green to chocolate brown, and wispy spikes of small pinkish blooms in spring.

EVERGREEN CANDYTUFT (Iberis sempervirens) Tidy, short perennial with shiny dark leaves most of the year that nearly disappear under an explosion of white blooms come spring. 'Snowflake' is particularly floriferous.

FESCUE (Festuca) Dense tufts of narrow, fine leaves in blue-gray or silvery shades. Compatible with most garden styles from traditional to minimalist modern. *F. glauca* 'Elijah Blue' is popular not just for its color but also for its longevity. *F. idahoensis*, a Western native, is slightly taller and more blue-green.

JAPANESE SWEET FLAG (Acorus gramineus) An evergreen grasslike plant with fragrant leaves. Golden yellow 'Ogon' and white-striped 'Variegatus' are more popular than the species. Likes moist soil. Pretty rimming a pond or stream.

❶ *Sedum spectabile* 'Neon'
❷ Licorice mint (*Agastache rupestris*)
❸ *Geranium* 'Rozanne'
❹ *Gaillardia* x *grandiflora* 'Oranges & Lemons'
❺ *Bidens ferulifolia*
❻ *Rudbeckia hirta* 'Denver Daisy'
❼ *Salvia leucantha* 'Santa Barbara'
❽ *Penstemon heterophyllus* 'Margarita BOP'

≈ Smart Choices ≈
SEASONAL ACCENTS

Some plants herald the seasons at full volume. A low-key perennial suddenly unfurls spring flowers, or a low, mounding ornamental grass shoots out blond flower spikes twice its height come summer, or a quiet green shrub might cover itself with clusters of cheerful winter berries. The following plants insist that you celebrate each season.

BERRIES

Bright berries are welcome garden ornaments in cold weather, when little is in bloom. They lure in bird visitors too, another plus.

MAHONIA Hollylike foliage of these shrubs is showy enough, but yellow flowers followed by equally ornamental blue-black fruit are striking bonuses. Oregon grape (*M. aquifolium*), a Northwest native; M. 'Golden Abundance'; and California holly grape (*M. pinnata*) are midsize varieties (to 5 feet tall) that thrive in most zones (except low desert) and need little supplemental water. For small spaces, choose lower-growing kinds such as M. a. 'Compacta', to 3 feet tall, and foot-tall creeping mahonia (*M. repens*). All have spiny-edged leaves, so situate them away from paths. Or try M. 'Soft Caress', which has no prickles and stays low.

PYRACANTHA These easy-going evergreen shrubs produce clusters of small white spring flowers followed in winter by a profusion of red-orange berries. *P. coccinea* 'Kasan' (8 to 10 feet tall) makes a good backdrop for borders; P. 'Red Elf' forms a low mound to 2 feet tall and wide; grow it toward the front of a border.

STRAWBERRY TREE (Arbutus unedo 'Elfin King') Small tree reaching 5 feet tall. Continuously bears white or greenish white flowers along with yellow and red berries that attract birds.

TOYON (Heteromeles arbutifolia) A handsome but low-key native California shrub with glossy, dark, leathery leaves and small white summer flowers followed by red winter berries that birds relish.

SEASONAL FLOURISHES

Certain flowers are seasonal essentials—gardeners have been planting these show-offs for eons, with good reason.

CANNA Although they need regular water during growth and bloom, cannas are easy to grow in warm climates, and worth it for their vivid "stained glass" leaves and fluttery flowers that add zip to borders and patio pots. Especially showy: 'Pretoria', with yellow-striped green leaves and orange blossoms; 'Tropicanna', with hot orange blooms above purple leaves striped with yellow, pink, and red; and 'Black Knight', with deep bronzy chocolate leaves and red blooms.

CROCOSMIA Tubular flowers on tall stems have hot colors—red-orange, orange, yellow. Named hybrids, such as 'Emily McKenzie' (orange flowers with red eyes), are especially showy.

DAHLIA These tuberous rooted perennials come in a rainbow of flower colors to accent summer borders. For the front row, black-leafed varieties, such as the 'Mystic' series or orange-flowered 'Bishop of Llandaff', are hard to beat. Choose varieties that will enhance your border's existing color scheme.

DAYLILY (Hemerocallis) Trumpet-shaped flowers on tall stems rise above clumps of sword-shaped leaves starting midspring. They come in sunny yellows and every other color too, including bicolors and blends. For a longer show, plant repeat bloomers.

EUPHORBIA CHARACIAS WULFENII
Big chartreuse flowers wake up the garden in early spring and fade very slowly. Caution: Milky white sap can be irritating on contact. Pretty beside Spanish lavender.

LILY-OF-THE-NILE (Agapanthus)
Flowers in white or a shade of blue form spherical clusters atop tall stems every spring or summer. All varieties are winners, but 'Midknight Blue' has the darkest blue flowers.

SEED HEADS

The tawny seed heads of dormant ornamental grasses and some shrubs capture the essence of autumn, when their buff hues complement the reds and oranges of changing leaves.

APACHE PLUME (Fallugia paradoxa) This high-country native produces small white roselike flowers spring through summer, then has long plumes of feathery seed heads late summer into fall.

BLUE GRAMA (Bouteloua gracilis 'Blond Ambition') Tough, heat- and drought-tolerant grass whose oddly attractive seed heads point outward like wind socks in a stiff breeze.

DROPSEED (Sporobolus) A graceful, fine-textured grass with plume-like flowers that create a hazy effect in fall. Great in meadows and mixed borders.

GIANT FEATHER GRASS (Stipa gigantea) Airy sheaves form a shimmering blond cloud.

INDIAN RICE GRASS (Oryzopsis hymenoides) Southwest native, to 2 feet tall, with open, airy, golden flower clusters.

MUHLENBERGIA CAPILLARIS 'RUBY MIST'
A mounding grass that sports gauzy pink clouds above it when in bloom. Spectacular when backlit.

REED GRASS (Calamagrostis) Dry flower spikes of *C. x acutiflora* 'Karl Foerster' shoot straight up from the plant like golden arrows. Pure drama.

SHOW-OFF CACTUS

Cactus are grown more for their architectural shapes than their flowers, but some put on quite a display.

HEDGEHOG CACTUS (Echinocereus engelmannii) Cylindrical, ribbed bodies form clumps 1 to 2 feet tall. Showy lavender to deep purple flowers are followed by red fruits.

OCOTILLO (Fouquieria splendens) Most of the year, ocotillo looks more like a wire sculpture than a plant—tall, thin, gray, furrowed, thorny stems. But when rain falls, green leaves and tubular red flowers seem to sprout overnight.

OPUNTIA Handsome sculptural plants with oval pads studded with decorative spines sport big, bright flowers come spring. *O. basilaris* and *O. aurea* have magenta flowers; *O. macrocentra* 'Tubac', yellow and red.

❶ *Crocosmia*
❷ *Dahlia* 'Hugs 'N' Kisses'
❸ *Opuntia aurea* 'Coombe's Winterglow'
❹ *Calamagrostis x acutiflora* 'Karl Foerster'
❺ *Euphorbia characias wulfenii*
❻ *Ocotillo (Fouquieria splendens)*
❼ *Arbutus unedo*
❽ *Toyon (Heteromeles arbutifolia)*

Succulents

COLOR ECHOES
▶

Euphorbia mauritanica's profusion of yellow flowers repeats the yellow margins of the *Agave attenuata* behind it. Gold-leafed *Crassula*, right of the agave, adds a second pool of warmth, and 'Blue Glow' agave, in front, a splash of cool. The succulents' beautiful geometric forms are more like sculptures than plants.

PERFECT BALANCE
◀

Muted greens and deep burgundies are in complete harmony in this circular garden retreat in Menlo Park, California, whose twin beds extend the curves of a stacked bluestone wall. A colony of wonderfully leggy *Aeonium arboretum* 'Zwartkop' rises above rock purslane (*Calandrinia spectabilis*), blue pickle (*Senecio mandraliscae*), and blue fescue (*Festuca glauca*), in front, echoing the hues of a potted *Loropetalum* 'Purple Pixie' and a bronze flax (*Phormium tenax* 'Atropurpureum'). A silvery green hedge of *Pittosporum tenuifolium* 'Marjorie Channon' adds a softening fringe behind the wall. DESIGN Lauren Dunec Hoang

Succulents are among the easiest plants you can grow. Superbly adapted to arid climates, they can survive with little or no supplemental irrigation, and they rarely need fertilizer. Just give them good drainage and a relatively mild winter (the majority are not very cold-hardy), and let them be. They really do thrive on neglect.

In fact, these tough plants have evolved, over centuries, with features that allow them to thrive in dry climates—thick, waxy leaves in tight rosettes that soak up and store water, or enlarged columnar or barrel-shaped stems that do the same. Their shallow root systems fit nicely into tiny planting pockets, green wall frames, and containers.

BOLD

Intensely colored garden walls command you to notice them, and you can't help but respond. Don't waste those theatrical backdrops by planting wimps in front. Vivid walls demand strong plants that can make their own statement. Big sculptural succulents fit the bill.

RHYTHMIC REPETITION

▲

A threesome of century plants (*Agave americana*) show off their fanlike habits and blue-green leaves against a cherry red wall in Arizona. A pair of mesquite trees (*Prosopis juliflora*) spread their canopies overhead. DESIGN Steve Martino

SHARP CONTRAST

◄

The cool green color and vertical form of *Cereus peruvianus* make this cactus the perfect foil for a wide expanse of tomato red wall in Phoenix. C. *peruvianus* can spread to 10 feet tall and 15 feet wide at maturity, so this contrast will get even more striking with time. A trio of blue rosettes (*Agave ovatifolia*), some feathery grass (*Nassella tenuissima*), and a mound of soft *Dalea capitata* round out the planting. DESIGN Chad Robert

LINE DRAWING

▲

A pair of ocotillos (*Fouquieria splendens*) in front of a mustard-colored wall in Arizona create the illusion of a giant abstract painting. Later, when bright green leaves sprout along the stems and red-orange flowers appear on top like candle flames, the golden background will make those colors pop. DESIGN Steve Martino

SUBTLE

Though succulents show off with aplomb against vivid walls, they look just as good against more subdued surfaces. A smooth backdrop of soft coral or pale blue allows the succulents' distinct geometric forms and contours to stand out more sharply than they would against rougher brick or wood. Flamboyant aloes against dark plum or chocolate-hued walls create pure drama.

SOFTENING EFFECT

▶

Two kinds of prickly pear—*Opuntia ficus-indica* and *Opuntia engelmannii* x *linguiformis*—look less bristly when placed in front of a beige-pink wall; the near-neutral, face-powder color even manages to tame the barrel cactus. The raised bed in this Tucson planting ensures good drainage, while the mesquite tree (*Prosopis chilensis*) provides dappled shade.

SOPHISTICATED PALETTE

▶

A few titans share a temporary mat of gold—blossoms from a palo verde tree—in front of an expanse of grape- and eggplant-colored walls in Phoenix. In front is an *Aloe vera*; behind it are two octopus agave (*A. vilmoriniana*). Several smaller agave fill in below. DESIGN Steve Martino

DYED-TO-MATCH

◀

A warm pink wall in Rancho Santa Fe, California, complements the fiery tips of *Euphorbia tirucalli* 'Sticks of Fire' and contrasts with the muscular tall, green *Euphorbia* behind it. The pair's cool companions are blue-gray *Cotyledon orbiculata* and *Festuca glauca* grass.

BOTANICAL MANDALA

◄

The foliage of X *Mangave* 'Espresso' in a Tucson garden is so ornamental—gray-green overall, ivory margins, bronze centers, rosy freckles—that appreciating it properly is a meditation exercise in itself. Purple lantana (*L. montevidensis*) accents the *Mangave*'s dark centers without competing with it for attention.

SERENE SIMPLICITY

Succulents are compelling to look at, especially when they are widely spaced so you can appreciate each plant's special beauty. A single beefy agave or aloe can produce the same effect if you set it beside a patio or bench as an accent or nestle it among lacy flowers and foliage. The understated plantings pictured here have a calm, reflective quality.

PAUSE MAKER

◀

Japanese gardens use chunky boulders at transitional points as a device to force visitors to slow down physically, which in turn slows them down mentally. Here, at the edge of a small dining alcove tucked into a corner of a Venice, California, garden, a single agave (*A. attenuata*) serves the same function. A privacy screen of bamboo (*Bambusa multiplex* 'Alphonse Karr') furthers the Zen-like feeling.
DESIGN Steve Siegrist

SEASCAPE

▲

Though succulents are the most static of plants, this scene in San Francisco seems to have the mesmerizing ebb and flow of the ocean. Tiny rosettes of mixed *Echeveria* and clumping lime-green *Sedum rupestre* 'Angelina', widely spaced and surrounded by a pebble mulch, look like anemones on the sea floor. A reedy *Chondropetalum tectorum*, reminiscent of kelp, behind, appears to move with the currents.

RAISED BEDS

Succulents are perfect for growing in raised bed plantings. They're evergreen—or, for that matter, ever-red, ever-orange, or ever-blue. Create a color scheme based on their striking foliage colors and enjoy it year-round. The plants' clean architectural shapes look good with virtually any style home but seem custom-made for simple, contemporary ones.

GRAPHIC DESIGN

◀

The strong shapes and emphatic colors of succulents make them natural landscaping choices for minimalist contemporary architecture. Their fleshiness adds some welcome softness too. Fishhook senecio (*S. radicans*) drapes from both planters in this Shell Beach, California, garden and shares space in each with *Senecio mandraliscae*. A tangle of purple heart (*Tradescantia pallida* 'Purpurea') provides a ribbon of contrasting color. DESIGN Jeffrey Gordon Smith

LUSH AND LAYERED

▲

Wide raised beds can have all the visual complexity of a mixed border. This one, in Rancho Santa Fe, California, shows off blue *Senecio mandraliscae*, prostrate rosemary, and a big blue *Agave attenuata* against the backdrop of a thick-trunked bottle tree (*Beaucarnea recurvata*).

STALWART SENTINELS

▲

Yuccas are tough plants, capable of withstanding harsh sunlight and heat reflecting off white walls. They tolerate hard frosts to boot. The two species pictured here stand guard at a front entrance in Tucson: *Y. rostrata* in the bottom planter, *Y. filamentosa* in the top. Mexican fence post (*Pachycereus marginatus*) adds to the vertical interest. Prostrate rosemary's drape contributes softness, as does the front edge of *Vinca major*. DESIGN Scott Calhoun

LIVING
PICTURES

If color is your inspiration when designing a garden, you have to love succulents. Few plants provide such a range of foliage hues to select from, and you know that the colors are good for the year, not just a season. All you have to do to create a beautiful scene is select compatible colors, just as an artist would pigments. Then paint away.

CLOSE HARMONY

◄

Succulent leaf colors are like nothing else on the planet— the iciest blues, rosiest corals, apple greens, even lavender. Here, a ruffle-skirted *Echeveria* 'Ballerina' and an assortment of small succulents, most in cool blues and jade green, show off their colors against a lacy, silvery-white cushion bush (*Leucophyta brownii*).

SPLASH OF LIME

►

A judicious jolt of yellow-green foliage brightens any color scheme, and few plants stay as consistently chartreuse as *Sedum rupestre* 'Angelina'. Here it warms up the red-violet leaves of a bayberry (*Berberis thunbergii* 'Crimson Pygmy').

GENTLE CONTRAST

►

A colony of blue-leafed *Echeveria secunda glauca* looks twice as cool with the yellow flower sprigs of pork and beans (*Sedum x rubrotinctum*) poking through here and there. The sedum's red tips also play up the lipstick pink edges of the aeonium.

PATTERNS

If you are drawn to patterns, whether in carpeting, wall covering, or fabrics, concentrate on arranging your succulents by shapes instead of by color. Pair big rosettes with smaller ones, starburst shapes with tufted jelly bean types. Move them around as though you're designing an abstract mosaic until you get an effect you like.

VARIATIONS ON A THEME

Most of the plants in this coastal Southern California vignette are *Echeveria*: the large blue rosette, *E. x imbricata*; the lavender rosettes around it, *E. 'Perle Von Nürnberg'*; and the smaller blue rosettes, *E. secunda* (with narrow, pointy-tipped leaves) and *E. x imbricata* (with slightly broader, more rounded tips). The smallest, orange plants are *Graptoveria 'Copper Roses'*. Although all are similarly shaped, the differences in sizes as well as colors keep the pattern interesting.

LUSH BOUQUET

▶

The lavender-pink rosettes of *Echeveria* 'Afterglow' and the serrated-edged lime *Aloe dorotheae* are the focal points of this tapestry in Corona del Mar, California. But it is the fillers—burgundy *Sedum spurium* 'VooDoo', ice-blue *Senecio serpens*, and an aqua-blue sedum—that make them pop.

ILLUSION OF MOTION

▶

The toothy curves of red Sunset aloe (*A. dorotheae*) in this Southern California garden look like pin-wheels spinning in the breeze. A pair of *Echeveria*—lavender 'Afterglow' and blue-green 'Fire and Ice'—seem to rein them in. Lime *Sedum rupestre* 'Angelina' and blue *Senecio serpens* fill in.

MONOCHROME WITH PUNCH

Gardens composed entirely of all green or all blue plants can make you feel blissfully serene, but they can also put you to sleep. The secret is to add some plants with dramatic presence to wake things up. Bringing in a few bold succulents, carefully placed, is an easy solution.

GLACIAL MEDLEY

▼

All the plants in this Pasadena, California, garden have strong personalities. But their close color harmony keeps everything mellow. Blue *Senecio mandraliscae* edges the bed, with pride of Madeira (*Echium candicans*) about to open its bluish purple flowers behind, and blue agave (*A. americana*) in the rear. The green exclamation in the middle is Mexican grass tree (*Dasylirion longissimum*).

AQUA DOTS

▲

One plant—*Agave parryi truncata*—provides the whole show in this California Central Coast garden. The fact that these agaves are not a uniform size, that they are widely separated on their decomposed gravel base, and that they are asymmetrically arranged makes the planting amusing. DESIGN Ryan Fortini

BLUE BURSTS

▲

Broad blades of *Agave americana* contrast with the delicate, needlelike leaves of *Rosmarinus* 'Collingwood Ingram'. Yet the agave's blue-gray hue complements the rosemary's. The water needs of the two plants match as well. Both get by on little irrigation but look more handsome given a bit more.

LIME AND JADE

Chartreuse foliage can wake up any planting—even soft jade blue. Try setting blue-green *Sedum ewersii* between pavers of a small garden path, along with chartreuse ornamental oregano (*Origanum vulgare* 'Aureum'). Both are low-growing groundcovers, and they'll soon ramble together in delicious ways as in this Seattle garden. Result: a planting as pretty as a bouquet, even without flowers. DESIGN Stacie Crooks

COOL AND CRUNCHY

◀

Some succulents seem particularly juicy, cooling off everything around them, and blue pickle (*Senecio mandraliscae*) is one of them. Here it forms a soft skirt around a stately variegated *Agave americana*. Italian cypress and a yucca provide a dark background.
DESIGN Amelia B. Lima

PRICKLY PARTNERS

▶

A dense colony of *Aloe x nobilis*—whose leaf edges have tiny white bristles— plays up the larger teeth of the blue agave hovering over them. *A. x nobilis* forms tight clumps of red-tinged rosettes and produces orange flowers in summer.

BREEZY COMPANIONS

◀

A meadow of sedge (*Carex pansa*) and wild rye (*Elymus canadensis*) surrounds the giant rosettes of *Agave americana* in this beachfront garden in Malibu, California. The grasses add contrasting texture and lots of motion, especially in this windswept location, and will also hide the gaps that occur when individual agaves eventually bloom and die.
DESIGN John Greenlee

CARPETING

Even giants want company. Huge agaves such as century plant (*A. americana*), tree aloes, and other imposing succulents can look isolated standing alone. Surrounding them with a living carpet of something shorter and softer not only grounds them—it makes them look more impressive.

TEAM
PLAYERS

Because of their endless range of fantastic shapes and colors, it is easy to fill a garden entirely with succulents. Not that there's anything wrong with that. But succulents are also happy to share space with a multitude of drought-tolerant companions, including grasses, trees, vines, and wildflowers.

CLASSIC SOUTHWEST DUO

◀

The sculptural shape of prickly pear cactus *(Opuntia engelmannii)* provides some structure against a backdrop of a freewheeling lantana so vigorous it is behaving like a vine in this Arizona garden.
DESIGN Steve Martino

BEVY OF BEAUTIES

▲

A pair of agaves *(A. attenuata)* hold their own among equally showy competitors, including violet-blue *Echeveria* 'Afterglow', ruby-spiked *Cordyline* 'Electric Pink', silver-and-burgundy-striped *Astelia nivicola* 'Red Gem', and pink-tipped *Leucadendron* 'Safari Sunset' in an El Cerrito, California, garden.
DESIGN Reynolds-Sebastiani

TIPS from a PRO

At Succulent Gardens wholesale and retail nursery in Castroville, California, ROBIN STOCKWELL grows more than 400 varieties of succulents; and he is always trying out fresh ways to use them.

EXPERIMENT

Don't overthink your design or worry about which plants go together—"succulents are all pretty compatible."

CONTRAST

Successful plantings really show off textures and colors in play with one another. Surround big blue rosettes of *Echeveria* x *imbricata* with smaller pink sedums, for example.

TEND

Low maintenance doesn't mean no maintenance. Succulents do require care, especially in containers. They need fast-draining soil, water (once every one to two weeks for a mature plant in a 4-to-6-inch pot), and sunlight. "But they're far more forgiving than other plants."

SHOW-OFFS

Succulents can be subtle, but, let's face it, it's not the modest ones that make you drop your jaw. It's the divas. Though these theatrical plants don't appear as if they want to share the stage with other succulents, in truth they look even more awesome when they do.

DUELING IDOLS

◄

A trio of golden barrel cactus (*Echinocactus grusonii*) compete for attention with a colony of rose-blushed, sharp-toothed *Aloe elgonica*. A second aloe, red-flowered *A. cameronii;* blue *Senecio mandraliscae;* and chartreuse elephant's food (*Portulacaria afra*) act as mediators in this Solana Beach, California, garden. DESIGN Jeff Moore

ON THE MOVE

►

A parade of red aloes (*Aloe cameronii*) appears ready to charge over a speed bump of boulders. Their irregular shapes provide a lively counterpoint to their companions, golden barrel cactus and blue agave, which look more static, like bystanders, in this Southern California garden.

YIN AND YANG

►

Echeveria subrigida 'Fire and Ice' and *Agave parryi* make excellent partners in a Northwest garden. The *Echeveria's* broad, soft-edged leaves and flowerlike form appear soft and frilly next to the agave's more upright, sharp-toothed foliage. Yellow-flowered *Sedum spathulifolium* 'Cape Blanco', lower left, along with hen and chicks (*Sempervivum* 'Ruby Heart') and Oregon stonecrop (*Sedum oreganum*), completes the circle. DESIGN Stacie Crooks

SPECIAL EFFECTS

Succulents are so different from all other plants that they sometimes look other-worldly. Take advantage of that. Use them to mimic a seafloor or tidepool or to create a fantasy garden that only exists in your mind. A lunar jungle, perhaps.

TIDEPOOL GARDEN

▼

These succulents look like sea creatures revealed in rocky pools at low tide. A striped agave (*A. americana* 'Medio-picta Alba') is the star of this cliff-edge border in a Corona del Mar, California, garden. Yellow-orange *Euphorbia tirucalli* 'Sticks on Fire' rise like coral behind it, while lavender-pink *Echeveria* 'Afterglow' and the crablike red aloes (*A. cameronii*) grow in front. Various sedums fill in around them.
DESIGN Joe Stead

JUNGLE FANTASY

▲

As lush as the Amazon but thriving on only a fraction of its rain, this San Diego garden looks like a jungle from another planet. A river of gray *Dymondia margaretae* weaves its way toward a giant century plant (*Agave americana*) at the crest of the garden. Along its banks, on the right, are blue-green *Aloe striata* and pinkish gray *Graptopetalum paraguayense;* on the left, pork and beans (*Sedum x rubrotinctum*) and blue *Senecio mandraliscae.* DESIGN Debra Lee Baldwin

SCUBA DIVER'S VIEW

▶

Rosy-pink rosettes of *Echeveria* nestle like sea anemones in a pebbly mat of blue *Senecio serpens.* The starfishlike creatures to their left are *Aeonium* 'Sunburst'. The tiny stars at bottom are *Crassula capitella thyrsiflora* 'Shark's Tooth'.

DYNAMIC DUOS

Although succulents can be combined with a wide array of other plants, there is a reason you tend to see the same pared-down designs time after time. Golden barrel cactus and blue agaves are a classic example; they always look good together. Here are others.

SUN-CATCHER

◄

The snow leopard chollas (*Cylindropuntia whipplei*) cover themselves with numerous white spines that positively glow in sunlight. Together they create a lacy effect behind pink-flowered beavertail cactus (*Opuntia basilaris*) in a Colorado garden. (Situate this cholla carefully, though, as its spines are treacherous.) The stones in front, softened with a patch of pink-flowered ice plant (*Delosperma* 'Kelaidis'), form a protective barrier.

CLASSIC COMBO

▲

Bougainvillea and agaves, both very drought-tolerant once established, are favored partners in Western gardens. In this San Diego–area planting, the agave (*A. americana*) is a cooling complement to a vivid *Bougainvillea* 'San Diego Red', one of the hardiest and most vigorous varieties.

TWO TO TANGO

A pair of saguaros (*Carnegiea gigantea*), the signature cactus of the Sonoran desert, may have started life as small knobs atop the desert soil. But they grew together, very slowly as saguaros do, only one foot every 10 years. Now this dancing pair, joyously youthful though they appear, are most likely centenarians—elegant and majestic—stealing the spotlight from all nearby plants. Find small potted saguaros for your desert garden at cactus specialty nurseries or botanical garden plant sales.

ᲤDesign ElementᲤ
CONTRAST

Contrast happens when you plant big-leafed varieties next to smaller-leafed ones, rough-textured leaves next to fine-textured ones, spiky plants next to wispy ones, bulbous next to skinny, or low, spreading next to upright. Pairing plants to play up their differences adds interest and punch, especially to beds and borders made up entirely of foliage plants.

Happily, succulents come in so many colors, leaf sizes, shapes, heights, and habits that you can easily combine them to play up all these differences at once, with striking effects. You can even create magical illusions in the process. The planting pictured here, for instance, recalls an undersea theme complete with wavy green kelp, giant sea anemones, and red crabs on the march.

SHAPES

Sea-themed succulents, from flat-topped to round to upright and delicate, fill this Southern California beachside border. They include (clockwise from top left) green *Senecio vitalis*; gray artichoke-shaped *Agave parryi truncata*; spiky and spotted X *Mangave* 'Bloodspot'; red, crablike aloe hybrids; caramel-colored pork and beans (*Sedum x rubrotinctum*); pink-tinged, icy blue paddle plant (*Kalanchoe luciae*), behind the aloes; and red-tipped *Crassula capitella thyrsiflora* 'Campfire'. DESIGN Joe Stead

BEAUTIFUL MIX-UPS

Because they are such distinctive plants, succulents might seem too exotic to include in mixed flower beds. But, actually, they make stellar accents among finer-foliaged plants. Their textures provide a starchy contrast to the softer foliage of shrubs, perennials, and grasses. Succulents pair handsomely with other drought-tolerant plants and most tolerate moderate watering regimens if planted in well-draining soil.

BRIGHT BOWL

◄

Where space is limited, pot up a mix of succulents to display on a deck or patio. Here, pink-tinged *Echeveria* (bottom), ice blue *E.* 'Ruffles' (top left), and purple-pink *E.* 'Perle von Nurnberg' (right) anchor the composition in a low bowl. Smaller succulents fill the gaps, including knobby green *Crassula ovata* 'Gollum'; gray-pink rosettes of *Graptopetalum pentandrum*; and yellow-green *Sedum rupestre* 'Angelina'. DESIGN Lauren Dunec Hoang

FOLIAGE REIGNS

◀

Leaves provide ample color all on their own in this Los Gatos, California, garden. A trio of agaves—two small *Agave attenuata* 'Nova' and big steely blue *Agave weberi*—stand out against a reddish purple smoke tree (*Cotinus coggygria*). A wispy blue fescue (*Festuca glauca*) adds a softening fringe in front. DESIGN Jarrod Baumann

HANDSOME BLEND

▲

Nearly everything in this wild tangle of succulents and evergreen perennials in a Waimea, Hawaii, garden is of South African origin. That includes the blue *Senecio mandraliscae* and red *Kalanchoe luciae* in the foreground, orange *Euphorbia tirucalli* 'Sticks on Fire', blue-green *Aloe arborescens* in the middle, and yellow pincushion plant (*Leucospermum* 'High Gold') in back.

GLACIAL COOL

▶

A generous river of icy blue *Senecio mandraliscae* weaves past islands of *Leucadendron* 'Wilson Red' and yellow-striped *Dietes iridioides* 'Variegata' in a Southern California garden. Rosy pink walls and red New Zealand flax *(Phormium)* add warming contrast behind. DESIGN Amelia B. Lima

BEACH GRASS
▼

A narrow-leafed Senecio
(*S. cylindricus*) spilling over
stone suggests a shoreline,
especially with a low white
groundcover *(Raoulia
australis)* rambling about at
its feet like sea foam. Black
mondo grass *(Ophiopogon
planiscapus* 'Nigrescens')
joins the mix, creating the
effect of wet kelp.

GROWING SUCCULENTS

Whether you're planting
a bed filled with mixed
succulents or a single
succulent in a patio pocket,
here's how to get them
off to the best start.

ENSURE GOOD DRAINAGE

Before planting, check
drainage by digging a hole
in the soil, about the size
of a 1-gallon pot, and filling
it with water. If the hole
takes more than four hours
to drain, dig in compost
and sharp sand or pumice
to improve texture. For
containers, use a packaged,
fast-draining cactus mix.

START BIG

In mixed beds, position the
largest and most dramatic
succulent first. Then place
the smaller succulents
around it, playing colors and
textures off one another
until you're pleased with the
arrangement, then plant. For
single-plant vignettes, place
a stone column in the bed,
then plant a dramatic rosette
at its base.

WATER

Once established, succulents
can survive on little or
sporadic watering, but that
doesn't mean they'll look
their best if they stay too
dry. Most will thrive with
a biweekly watering during
the active spring and
summer growing season.

179

POCKETS

Succulents do not have extensive root systems, so they don't need much soil to thrive. If you want to break up a walkway, deck, or patio with planting pockets to soften the look of an expanse of hardscape, these are the plants for the job. Some will even survive in tiny crevices in walls or wedged between boulders.

WARM WELCOME

A tree aloe (A. arborescens) on an elevated deck in Los Gatos, California, spreads its arching canopy over a cluster of warm-toned plants: coral aloe (A. striata), orange Libertia peregrinans—a sword-leafed plant in the iris family—and golden sedum.
DESIGN Jarrod Baumann

PEACEFUL PASSAGE

Cool blue Senecio mandraliscae, gray-green Agave attenuata, and the groundcover Dymondia margaretae create a soft border around a patio in a California Central Coast garden. The pocket garden also connects the space with the larger garden beyond.
DESIGN Ryan Fortini

CAREFREE COVER

▲

One type of plant, *Sedum dendroideum*, covers much of the slope of this drought-tolerant Oakland, California, front yard, though a little blue *Senecio mandraliscae* peeps out at the edges. The sedum's blaze of yellow flowers is particularly welcome when the garden's California buckeye (*Aesculus californica*) is leafless.

WAVES

Small-leafed succulents make excellent groundcovers, whether they appear to flow down a slope in broad swaths, ripple across the foreground of a planting bed, or wiggle through a tabletop trough.

ROOTING SUCCULENT CUTTINGS

Succulents are easy to root from offsets (pups) or cuttings. Just pull or snip them from the parent plant—ideally at the beginning of the spring growing season—and let the stem ends dry for a few days to harden (callus) them. Then plant.

▶ Pot one cutting or offset each per 2- or 4-inch pot. Moisten the mix.

▶ Set the pots in a warm, lightly shaded spot until the offsets take root (in about a month). Wiggle the plants lightly to check; if they don't move, they're rooted and ready to transplant into a bed, border, or larger mixed container.

TABLE RUNNER
▲

Small succulents in a long trough make an excellent centerpiece for an outdoor dining table—low enough that they don't impede eye contact but interesting enough to generate conversation. The two in front are *Sempervivum: S. soboliferum*, right; *S. arachnoideum*, left. Behind them are a pair of *Echeveria agavoides*, then *Sedum* 'Burrito'.
DESIGN Molly Wood

RIBBONS
▲

Different-hued succulents weave this tapestry in an Escondido, California, garden. They are (back to front) blue-gray *Oscularia deltoides* (formerly *Lampranthus deltoides*), orange-blushed *Crassula* 'Campfire', pale gray *Graptopetalum paraguayense*, and bright green *Sedum* x *rubrotinctum*.

⸻ *Design Element* ⸻
TEXTURE

Foliage textures mostly fall into three categories—fine, medium, and bold. You want all three textures in your garden. Pay special attention to fine and bold textures, since they're the mood-makers.

Feathery grasses add grace and movement, especially when mixed with wildflowers in cottage or naturalistic gardens. Many succulents, on the other hand, have corrugated spiny or rubbery-looking leaves that create a bolder effect. For an exotic or architectural look, use these types more generously. Feathery and bold combine especially well too.

Texture is a powerful but sometimes neglected tool. Don't forget to use it.

STRIPES

A ribbon of blue fescue (*Festuca glauca* 'Elijah Blue') separates two succulents: blue *Senecio talinoides* and bright green *Crassula capitella thyrsiflora* 'Campfire.' Besides changing texture, the grass adds movement to this garden in San Marino, California. DESIGN Darren Shirai and Jeremy Taylor

THE NATURALS

If you want a garden that feels like the desert, add some boulders. Succulents and stone are made for each other; huddled together, they create a "planted by nature" look. Or cluster plants, leaving bare stretches between them, the way they often grow in Southwest deserts, then cover the soil around them with a pretty mulch. Boulders make ideal backsrops.

ROUGH AND READY
▶

Aloe vera grows beside a boulder, with a weathered branch adding a sculptural accent between. The rocky mulch enhances the natural look.

DESERT CROWD
▶

Jewel aloe (*Aloe distans*) is aptly named: tiny golden teeth along the leaf margins give it a sparkle—even against a plain bark mulch back-drop. Plants spread by run-ning, rooting branching stems to form clumps of tight rosettes to 5 feet or more across. In sum-mer, they send up 2-foot-tall stems topped with clus-ters of rounded red flowers. This aloe is best in cooler locations, where it needs only occasional irrigation.

THE OPPORTUNISTS
◀

Groupings of *Senecio cylin-dricus* cluster around widely spaced boulders in a garden in Santa Barbara, looking as though they were planted there by wind-blown seed.
DESIGN Rob Maday

CACTUS JUNGLE

▼

Many forms of columnar cactus crowd together in the Desert Garden at Huntington Botanical Gardens in San Marino, California, like bystanders watching the Rose Bowl Parade on New Year's Day. Most belong to the genus *Cereus*. Beautiful when backlit by the sun, they're striking when massed. In a smaller garden, try a trio.

SCULPTURE GARDEN

▶

Because only a few species of plants are used in this Palm Springs, California, garden, each one stands out as an individual. Golden barrel cactus (*Echinocactus grusonii*), blue *Agave parryi truncata*, and the shaving brush heads of *Yucca rostrata* join a single columnar *Trichocereus pachanoi*. DESIGN Desert Landscape Design

FULL TILT
OR SPARE

If you want a minimalist garden, cactus and succulents are superb choices. Few other plants look as good in spare landscape designs. But succulents can just as easily go to the other extreme. You can use them to create the beautiful tangle of a traditional mixed border or incorporate them into orderly patterns.

CACTUS CARE

As tough as they appear, cactus can use a little care on occasion. To start, always plant spiny or prickly cactus away from paths, patios, and other gathering spots for people or pets.

▶ Wear long leather gloves when handling cactus to protect hands and arms from prickles or thorns.

▶ Protect cactus from severe frost, although many large specimens will tolerate night temperatures as low as 28° provided days are warm (the flesh absorbs enough heat to last through a nighttime chill).

▶ Cactus have shallow feeder roots, so pull weeds by hand to avoid disturbing the soil around them (don't hoe). Avoid using chemical weed killers.

▶ Use a soft whisk broom to clean low-growing barrel cactus of pebbles and windblown debris.

ACCENTS

Sometimes all it takes is succulents to make a nondescript section of a garden into a scene stealer. Pair a beautiful succulent with a block of basalt, an interesting boulder, or a spiky perennial, and you have created a mini focal point, turning a problem into a pleasure.

VIEW FINDER
◄

The vista from this elevated balcony in Pasadena is pleasant though not compelling. But the vignette of strong, sculptural plants provides a much more interesting tableau. The big green *Agave attenuata* is joined by a bronze flax *(Phormium)* and the near-black rosettes of *Aeonium arboreum* 'Zwartkop'. A pale *Echeveria* and rosy *Sedum* 'Vera Higgins' complete the picture.
DESIGN Heather Lenkin

PERFECT DRAINAGE
▲

Since the natural habitat of native California *Dudleya* is coastal cliffs or hilly out-croppings, this succulent is perfectly at home tucked between stones in a dry-stacked wall in a Morro Bay, California, garden. Blue sedge *(Carex flacca)* provides company below.
DESIGN Jeffrey Gordon Smith

SUPER BOWL

To lighten a pebbly patch beside a patio, try this: Fill a low bowl with an array of succulents in contrasting colors and leaf shapes. (The bowl should be at least 14 inches in diameter and 4 to 6 inches deep, with drainage holes in the bottom.) Partially fill the bowl with light, fast-draining cactus mix, set your plants atop the soil, move them around until you're happy with the design, then plant. Fill in with additional soil as needed. Here, light gray-green *Echeveria* x *imbricata* touches the tips of a rosy blue *Echeveria subrigida* 'Fire and Ice'. A tiny sedum *(S. hispanicum)* fills the gaps.
DESIGN Jeffrey Gordon Smith

TINY TABLEAU

▲

In a garden, the tightly packed rosettes of hen and chicks (*Sempervivum tectorum*) are often used as filler between larger succulents. But show them off in a cluster of small pots, and you have a striking centerpiece for a patio table. The plant in the foreground grows nicely in enough soil to fill a 4-inch nursery pot, with small stones packed around it, and a little gentle irrigation in the summer.
DESIGN Tish Treherne

CANDY BOWL

▲

Succulent cuttings make great instant arrangements to dress a table for an evening gathering. Snipped from established garden plantings, the ones pictured here fill a blue glass bowl (no water needed). Frilly, chartreuse *Sedum rupestre* 'Angelina' peeks out beneath pink and gray *Echeveria* circling the rim, and an icy blue-gray *Graptopetalum* fills the center. After a few days, the cut stems can be cured (hardened) and rooted in soil-filled nursery pots to grow a collection (see page 179 for tips).
DESIGN Johanna Silver

EYE CANDY

As useful as succulents are in gardens, you can appreciate them even more when you grow them in containers and place them where you can view them more closely—such as atop a patio table or beside an entry. Plant single specimens in small pots to appreciate their perfect geometry, or combine several species in a bowl to admire their play of colors and textures. Succulents make perfect finishing touches for evergreen plantings in large containers.

LIVING JEWELS

◄

Giant bird
of paradise
(*Strelitzia nicolai*)
looks dramatic
enough to show
off alone in this
Montecito,
California,
planting. But add
a collar of rosy
*Echeveria
agavoides* and
black *Aeonium
arboreum*
'Atropurpureum',
plus a drape
of fishhook
senecio (*Senecio
radicans*),
and the result
is positively
glamorous.
DESIGN
Zac Williams

SUCCULENTS *and* CACTUS

Succulents are the easiest, most striking plants you can grow. Some favorites and the best ways to use them are listed here. Most need only little to moderate water.

GARDEN ACCENTS

The following make striking focal points.

AGAVE The creamy stripes on leaves of *A. americana* 'Medio-picta Alba' are pure drama. Other beauties: 'Blue Flame', with mottled blue-green leaves; 'Blue Glow', with bluish leaves edged in red; dwarf butterfly agave (*A. potatorum* 'Kichijo-kan'), with gray-green leaves edged with deep red spines. *A. parryi truncata*, a powerhouse, looks like a giant artichoke.

ALOE When in bloom, torch aloe (*A. arborescens*) resembles a glowing candelabra. Cape aloe (*A. ferox*) sends up branches of showy red or orange blooms in late fall or winter; give it room. Or try 'Blue Elf', which forms a dense mound of 6-inch rosettes.

CALANDRINIA GRANDIFLORA Clumping plant 1 to 3 feet tall with thick, rounded, fleshy gray leaves; most effective when massed. Brilliant magenta blooms, which appear to float on slender stems in summer, are like icing on the cake.

FURCRAEA FOETIDA MEDIOPICTA Stripes of cream to green create a watercolor effect on the leaves.

MANGAVE 'Bloodspot' forms a compact, foot-tall rosette with upright, 8-inch leaves speckled in red. X M. 'Macho Mocha' is much bigger (4 to 6 feet wide).

TREE ALOE (A. barbarae) Mature specimens resemble palm trees, but with stiff, fleshy leaves.

BEDS AND BORDERS

Large rosettes add punch.

ALOE Red aloe (*A. cameronii*) grows 1 to 2 feet tall with narrow, upright leaves that turn coppery red in summer and bright orange-red flowers. Spider aloe (*A. x spinosissima*) has green leaves edged with pointy "teeth" and tall spikes of tubular, coral red blooms; it grows just 3 feet tall. Jeweled aloe (*A. distans*), a sprawler from South Africa, has deep green leaves edged with golden yellow teeth and coral blooms late summer to fall.

ECHEVERIA *E. agavoides* 'Lipstick' has green leaves flushed with red; *E. a.* 'Afterglow' has silvery blue leaves flushed with pink. Hen and chicks (*E. secunda*) form tight clumps of blue-green rosettes and red to yellow summer blooms—great for border edgings. *E. subrigida* 'Fire and Ice' has 18-inch-wide rosettes of spade-shaped bluish green leaves often highlighted with smooth, rosy brown edges.

GRAPTOPETALUM PARAGUAYENSE Ghostly gray, this thick-leafed native of Mexico forms a mound 8 inches tall. Pair it with hot-colored plants.

SEDUM Pacific stonecrop (*S. spathulifolium* 'Cape Blanco') is silvery gray with yellow flowers. Coppertone stonecrop (*S. nussbaunianum*) is low-growing (8 inches tall and 2 to 3 feet wide), with elongated rosettes of green and yellow, edged in burnt orange, and white flowers late winter to spring; it colors best with some water. *S. telephium* has clusters of showy rose to bronze flowers in fall.

SENECIO *S. mandraliscae* is a showy and popular rambler, to 18 inches tall, whose fleshy, blue fingerlike leaves make pretty edgings for borders. Blue chalksticks (*S. serpens*) is similar but smaller (a foot-tall ground hugger). *S. vitalis* has narrower green leaves with pointed tips.

GROUNDCOVERS

Tuck these between pavers or along paths.

HEN AND CHICKS (Echeveria elegans) Tight grayish white rosettes spread freely by offsets. Useful in pattern planting. Protect from hot summer sun.

SEDUM *S. makinoi* 'Ogon' has rounded yellow leaves. *S. sieboldii* has spreading blue-gray rosettes with red edges. *S. spurium* has dark green and bronze-tinted leaves.

CONTAINERS

Most succulents thrive in low bowls or in mixed plantings in big pots. The ones here are especially striking.

AEONIUM *A. arboreum* grows 3 feet tall and wide and forms 6-to-10-inch rosettes (depending on variety), so give it room. *A. a.* 'Atropurpureum' is magenta-green; 'Zwartkop', nearly black. *A.* 'Cyclops' forms rosettes of dark reddish bronze leaves on stems to 3 feet tall, with newest green leaves adding a green "eye" in the center. *A.* 'Sunburst' has 12-inch green rosettes variegated in light yellow; for a cooling summer combo, plant it with frilly 'Angelina' sedum. *Aeonium tabuliforme* has flat rosettes resembling waterlilies.

CRASSULA CAPITELLA THYRSIFLORA 'CAMPFIRE' Forms rosettes of fleshy, apple-green leaves edged with red that turn dark red in intense sun. Pretty in a glazed orange or apple green container; protect from frost.

EUPHORBIA TIRUCALLI 'STICKS ON FIRE' Pencil-thin stems resemble sea coral; they're pale green and pink, but turn fiery salmon in sun.

X GRAPTOVERIA 'FRED IVES' Big, with foot-wide clumps of large pinkish blue rosettes. Plant in a large bowl about 6 inches wide and at least 10 inches deep.

HENS AND CHICKS (Sempervivum) Small rosettes that make great fillers.

KALANCHOE *K. luciae* and *K. thyrsiflora* are similar. The former has large oval, gray-green leaves whose margins turn bright red in full sun; the latter, blue-green leaves with no red flush.

SEDUM Donkey tail (*S. morganianum*) is a bluish trailer; plant in an urn and let it spill. *S. m.* 'Burrito' has fatter tails. Use *S. rupestre* 'Angelina' to fringe pot edges.

ZEBRA PLANT (Haworthii fasciata) Small rosette-forming succulents with spiky leaves banded with raised white stripes. Forms dense clumps; best in mild climates.

SPECIAL EFFECTS

Cactus are technically succulents, but their needlelike spines set them apart.

BARREL CACTUS (Echinocactus) Prickly globes that grow slowly. Pretty with grassy *Libertia peregrinans* and coral aloes.

DWARF ORGANPIPE CACTUS (Stenocereus thurberi littoralis) Ribbed and spiny columns form clumps that resemble a pipe organ; grows slowly to 10 feet tall. Pink spring flowers.

OCOTILLO (Fouquieria splendens) Bare of foliage and flowers in summer, but always sculptural.

SNOW LEOPARD CHOLLA (Cylindropuntia whipplei) Also known as whipple cholla, this Southwest native is branching and bristly, but its long white thorns are beautiful when backlit. Plant it well away from paths.

❶ Pacific stonecrop (*Sedum spathulifolium* 'Cape Blanco')
❷ Cape aloe (*A. ferox*)
❸ Silvery *Graptoveria* with purple heart (*Tradescantia*)
❹ *Agave americana*
❺ *Furcraea foetida mediopicta*
❻ *Senecio talinoides thyrsiflora* (left); *Crassula capitella* 'Campfire' (right)
❼ *Aeonium* 'Cyclops'
❽ Golden barrel cactus (*Echinocactus*) with coral aloe (*A. striata*) and grassy *Libertia peregrinans*

Ground-covers

HOT PINK CARPET

◄

Bougainvillea 'Rosenka', a smaller variety, here pruned into a shrub, lines one side of stairs in a Santa Barbara garden (across from blue-flowered ceanothus on the opposite side). It provides nearly year-round color in this warm climate.
DESIGN Isabelle Greene

Matlike plants such as lawns constitute a tiny fraction of the broad groundcover category. Prostrate shrubs (ones that grow more horizontally than vertically) such as 'Yankee Point' ceanothus and rock cotoneaster—both ideal for covering slopes or large swaths of yard—are groundcovers too. So are the short, shrubby perennials such as thyme that look attractive spilling over onto pathways or edging borders. Low growers such as *Dymondia* soften and add permeability to pathways. They can also edge borders. Even in small meadows, ornamental grasses suggest wind-rippled prairie grass.

BLANKET OF BLUE

◄

'Yankee Point' ceanothus
(*C. griseus horizontalis*
'Yankee Point') covers most
of this Southern California
front yard. Its dense, glossy
foliage stays attractive year-
round, and the plant blooms
profusely with bright blue
flowers in the spring. Strawberry tree (*Arbutus* 'Marina'),
at right, which likes the
same dry conditions, makes
an excellent companion.
DESIGN Stephanie Wilson
Blanc

SPLASH OF LIME

▲

The yellow-green tips of
Juniperus chinensis 'Daub's
Frosted' lap at the ground
like waves splashing against
a rocky shore in this
Vancouver, Washington,
garden. Chartreuse flowers
of lady's-mantle (*Alchemilla
mollis*) repeat the color, and
a ribbon of red Japanese
blood grass (*Imperata
cylindrica* 'Rubra') provides
contrast.

DRAWING
A LINE

Clumping grasses and matlike groundcovers can
be shaped more precisely than low-growing hedges.
If you like to see clear patterns in your garden,
these are your best groundcover choices.

GREEN WEDGE

A triangle of woolly thyme (*Thymus serpyllum*) angles up to a pink-flowered thyme and a golden oregano, creating living geometry in a Novato, California, garden.

STRIPES

▲

Clumps of tufted hair grass (*Deschampsia cespitosa*) are lined up in neat rows reminiscent of farm crops in this Jackson, Wyoming, garden. The grass's foliage turns golden as the weather cools, just when the leaves of the garden's deciduous trees do.
DESIGN Bruce Greig and Greg Stewart

FRAMED

▲

An edging of blue fescue (*Festuca glauca* 'Elijah Blue') surrounds a bed of purple heart (*Tradescantia pallida* 'Purpurea') in a San Marino, California, garden, creating the illusion of a second pool.
DESIGN Darren Shirai and Mark Mariano

TIPS from a PRO

JOHN GREENLEE, an expert in grass ecology and sustainable design, and author of *The American Meadow Garden* and *The Encyclopedia of Grasses,* has created meadows for the San Diego Zoo, Disney's Animal Kingdom, and the Getty Center in Los Angeles, and in private gardens around the world.

THE RIGHT GRASS

Best are low, clumping drought-tolerant types, such as blue grama (*Bouteloua gracilis* 'Blond Ambition') and dropseed (*Sporobolus*). Plant them in widely spaced clusters, with room to grow. Water deeply to establish, then slowly wean them off the water.

ACCENTS

Grasses and succulents make great pairs—"architectural meets breezy." Cluster aloes among the grasses. Tuck in a few flowering plants—orange *Crocosmia,* for example. But keep the planting simple; "too many colors and textures can ruin the effect."

LIQUID EFFECTS

Groundcovers are most often thought of as sensible, utilitarian plants. But low-growing types can play more fanciful roles as well. Just like taller plants, they can be used as green graphics or as low, textured "pause points" between taller, bushier plants.

RAPIDS

◄

Planted in curved rows, Japanese forest grass (*Hakonechloa macra* 'Aureola') suggests a fast-moving stream. The bright foliage lights up this shady Portland garden. DESIGN Karen Ford

STILL WATERS

◄

Though this shade garden in Portland is lushly planted with ferns, iris, and *Gunnera*, the slightly sunken area in the middle is only lightly covered with a layer of moss, creating the effect of a vernal pool near the end of its wet season. The dwarf mondo grass (*Ophiopogon japonicus* 'Nana') and golden *Acorus gramineus* 'Ogon' on its banks reinforce the illusion. DESIGN Matteucci-Kalbfleisch (homeowners)

SPLASHES

►

Most of the plants in this Phoenix backyard are contained within a serpentine steel planter. The one exception is *Euphorbia rigida*, the fleshy-leafed perennial with chartreuse flowers that pops up in random splashes throughout the decomposed granite, as if planted by nature. Though *E. rigida* reseeds generously, unwanted plants pull up easily. DESIGN Christy Ten Eyck

TAPESTRY

You can create an interesting garden entirely out of low-growing plants. The secret is to vary the heights of plants slightly and include lots of different textures, shapes, and flower colors that go well together. Add some grasses too—especially ones that dance in the breeze.

BEACHY BLEND

◄

A purple-flowered thyme (*Thymus serphyllum*) edges a path on Camano Island, Washington, that leads to a Puget Sound view. Also in flower are pink sea thrift (*Armeria maritima*), blue *Ceanothus impressus* 'Victoria', and yellow blanket flower (*Gaillardia* x *grandiflora*). Dwarf mugo pine (*Pinus mugo mugo* 'Slowmound'), 'Munstead' lavender, blue oat grass (*Helictotrichon sempervirens*), and miscanthus (*M. sinensis* 'Gracilis') add contrast.
DESIGN Scott Lankford

PRETTY PARTNERSHIP

▲

The blue fingers of *Senecio mandraliscae* spill out of a planting pocket near a fence in a Redwood City, California, garden. The dark green, swordlike leaves of kangaroo paw (*Anigozanthos*) add another layer of interest year-round and also contribute striking lemon-colored blooms spring through fall.
DESIGN Jared Vermeil

PATHS

Planting unthirsty groundcovers between pavers visually ties pathways with the rest of the garden. Perhaps more important, creating these planted spaces—instead of opting for more solid paving—helps rainfall percolate into the soil, so it stays on the property. If you want a lush, wild look, use this "green mortar" generously; for a more restrained look, use it sparingly. Pay attention to the path's edges as well, whether you fringe it with low sedums, as pictured here, or with pillowy grasses as shown on pages 208–209.

BANDS
▶

Broad strips of *Thymus serpyllum* 'Elfin' dissect a flagstone path in a Los Altos, California, garden. A dark green sedum encroaches on the left; a brighter lime green variety on the right.
DESIGN Rebecca Sweet

FLORAL CARPET
◀

Blue star creeper *(Pratia pedunculata)*, which spreads by runners, fills the spaces between pavers in a Grants Pass, Oregon, front yard and carpets the open ground between *Pennisetum orientale* and *Sedum* 'Autumn Joy'. Though tolerant of most soils, partial shade, and foot traffic, *P. pedunculata* is fairly thirsty, so it's not the best choice for arid parts of the West.
DESIGN Jim Love

FLECKS
▶

Thin ribbons of Irish moss *(Sagina subulata)* fill in the spaces between randomly cut pavers in a Jackson, Wyoming, garden. The fluff from cottonwood trees sticks to the moss, further softening the path.
DESIGN Bruce Greig and Greg Stewart

SWATHS
▶

New Zealand brass button *(Leptinella squalida)* tolerates light foot traffic and also somewhat shady conditions. It thrives in this cool Portland garden.
DESIGN Debbie Erickson and Nick Erickson

EDGINGS

Sometimes a graceful path needs a soft fringe to set it off. Choose groundcovers or low, mounding plants that take the same conditions and complement or contrast with nearby plantings.

WINTERY CHARMS
◄

A sweeping edge of black mondo grass (*Ophiopogon planiscapus* 'Nigrescens') adds a dash of mystery to a Bremerton, Washington, garden, especially during its quieter winter season. The pendulous flowers on the right belong to an ornamental filbert tree (*Corylus avellana* 'Contorta'); the white and pink flowers to *Viburnum* x *bodnantense*. On the left is a 'Ramapo' rhododendron, which complements the cinnamon hues of a deciduous *Stewartia monadelpha* tree.
DESIGN John Albers, Albers Vista Gardens

LAYERED EFFECT
▲

Chartreuse and burgundy never fail to look striking together. Here, the chartreuse comes from Japanese forest grass (*Hakonechloa macra* 'Aureola'), which looks even brighter spilling out beneath the deep burgundy leaves of purple fountain grass (*Pennisetum advena* 'Rubrum').

TUCK-INS

The ratio of hardscape to planted ground in gardens is changing. Bigger homes take over more of the lot and, as a result, there's often more paving than planting. Recurring droughts in much of the West make permeable paving practically essential. Creating niches in the hardscape where you can tuck in matlike groundcovers helps blur the division between hardscape and landscape, which softens everything.

SEAWORTHY

▲

Strips of *Dymondia margaretae* soften the flagstone paving of this California Central Coast garden. Besides being able to withstand salt spray, *Dymondia* has soft gray-green hues that match the colors of the sea and sky along this stretch of the coast. Pheasant's-tail grass (*Anemanthele lessoniana*), kangaroo paw (*Anigozanthos*), and *Phlomis fruticosa* fill the planter. DESIGN Jeffrey Gordon Smith

OUTCROPPING

◄

Proving how well it thrives on sharp drainage, woolly thyme (*Thymus serpyllum*) emerges from between boulders in a Bainbridge Island, Washington, garden. English lavender (*Lavandula angustifolia*) provides vertical contrast to the thyme's low, mounding form.

SOFT STEPS

◄

This cleverly planted South African groundcover, *Dymondia margaretae*, appears to trickle like water from step to step in a California Central Coast garden. Silvery *Echeveria* rosettes are tucked up against the step risers like stones. DESIGN Ryan Fortini

GREEN MORTAR

►

Thymus serpyllum 'Elfin' fills in between concrete pavers around the firepit seating area in a Los Osos, California, garden. Despite its lush appearance, 'Elfin' thyme is very drought-tolerant. Little mounds of sea thrift (*Armeria maritima*) add more softness. Mexican weeping bamboo (*Otatea acuminata aztecorum*) encloses the space. DESIGN Jeffrey Gordon Smith

GET GRAPHIC

You can soften hardscape with groundcover insets but still keep a modern look. Just use crisp geometric lines rather than more random, organic ones and create bold, graphic patterns.

SQUARES

▶

Borders of *Dymondia margaretae* around acid-washed concrete squares create a crisp windowpane check in a Cayucos, California, garden. *D. margaretae* is usually planted from plugs and grows rather slowly; allow six months or so for it to fill in this densely. *Leymus condensatus* 'Canyon Prince' forms a backdrop.
DESIGN Jeffrey Gordon Smith

RECTANGLES

◀

Strips of tall fescue form a Mondrian-esque graphic in a Manhattan Beach, California, garden. Because the pieces are the standard width of sod sold at garden stores, replacement of any single patch, should it prove necessary, will be easy. The exuberance of mat rush (*Lomandra longifolia*) in the Cor-ten steel planter provides a wild contrast.
DESIGN Mark Tessier

STRIPES

▶

Horizontal bands of green *Thymus serpyllum* 'Elfin', with puffs of flowering sedum at one end, make an inviting entry in a Tiburon, California, garden. The sedum's blooms echo the yellow flowers of kangaroo paws (*Anigozanthos*) growing inside and outside the gate.
DESIGN Gretchen Whittier

INSTEAD OF
THIRSTY LAWN

Lawn grass is simply too thirsty a choice for gardens in much of the West, now that water shortages and severe droughts are occurring all too frequently. Fortunately, there are many options that are both good-looking and unthirsty—some you can even walk on. You can choose a drought-tolerant, matlike groundcover or totally rethink your yard. Perhaps you would rather have a meadow, or a prairie, or a chic and architectural cactus display.

BACKYARD GRASSLANDS

◄

The prairie comes all
the way to the walls
in this Sunol, California,
property. Tall Atlas fescue
(*Festuca mairei*) is the
primary grass, with accents
of upright *Calamagrostis
x acutiflora* 'Karl Foerster'
and blue *Helictotrichon
sempervirens*. Yarrow
(*Achillea*) and lavender
fill the role of wildflowers.
DESIGN Joseph Huettl

CALMLY CENTERED

▼

A mat of gray *Dymondia
margaretae*, dotted with an
occasional island of green
Carex divulsa and 'Bronze
Carpet' sedum, recalls the
smooth greenish look of
a glacial lake in a Los Altos,
California, garden. The silver
tones of its leaves complement the pink Jupiter's beard
(*Centranthus ruber*), blue
penstemon (*P. heterophyllus*
'Blue Springs'), and silvery
white lamb's ears (*Stachys
byzantina*). Sweet peas
ramble up a trellis against
the back wall.
DESIGN Rebecca Sweet

A LITTLE
BIT WILD

If you want to get rid of your lawn, putting down a less thirsty carpet is one option.
Or you could rethink the whole space by filling it with less tailored plants. Create an
exuberant garden of regionally appropriate plants that look as if nature might have
scattered them in. Or play it safe and choose unthirsty grasses.

PERFECT PAIR

Ornamental grasses are striking enough to carry the show in front-yard gardens. But pair them with the right flowering shrubs, and magic happens. Here, showy purple fountain grass (*Pennisetum advena* 'Rubrum') bends its velvety blooms (which rarely if ever set seeds) over vivid orange and yellow lantana. Both prefer mild climates and take moderate water. The lantana blooms attract hummingbirds.

DESERT ABSTRACT

◄

A widely spaced grid of deer grass (*Muhlenbergia rigens*) under the light shade of mesquite trees (*Prosopis* 'Phoenix'), with a few blue agaves (*A. weberi*) as accents, creates the feeling of the desert in this Phoenix front yard but conveys it in a contemporary graphic way. The planters contain *Pedilanthus* and *Euphorbia*. DESIGN Christy Ten Eyck

LIGHT AND LACY

▲

Arid landscapes don't have to look barren, as this lush Los Angeles front yard demonstrates. Pride of Madeira (*Echium candicans*), the tall shrubs underneath the *Jacaranda mimosifolia* trees, are just beginning to erupt into an explosion of blue. Clumps of orange-flowered *Bulbine frutescens*, right, contribute to the show. Twin agaves flank the pathway, and a line of *Phormium,* behind the fence, adds structure. DESIGN Michelle Merrill (homeowner)

FLOWER
POWER

If you prefer to replace your lawn with color, there are many
unthirsty options. Arrange flowering plants in jumbles of vivid
color rather than strictly by height. You'll have an eye-catching
garden that you may find more interesting than using grass alone.

NATIVE CHARMS

▶

While many gardens go dormant in the heat of late summer, this front yard in Venice, California, explodes with the red-orange blooms of 'Catalina' California fuchsia (*Zauschneria*). The flower, which grows naturally in rocky areas or on dry slopes, thrives with little irrigation. DESIGN Jeff Pervorse

SUMMER SPLENDOR

◀

Black mondo grass (fringing the rock), yellow-tinged *Sedum rupestre* 'Angelina', and a big-leafed *Bergenia cordifolia* 'Bressingham Ruby', edge this planting in Shoreline, Washington. Rising behind are pink hydrangea and chocolate-leafed *Physocarpus opulifolius* 'Diabolo'. *Rudbeckia fulgida sullivantii* 'Goldsturm' shows off yellow blooms in the center. At left is a tall Kousa dogwood, at right gold-tinted *Cupressus sempervirens* 'Swane's Golden'. DESIGN Stacie Crooks

COLORFUL WELCOME

▲

Blue catmint (*Nepeta* x *faassenii*) and yellow yarrow (*Achillea* 'Moonshine') planted en masse on either side of a curving walkway put on an exuberant show in a Santa Fe front yard. Red valerian (*Centranthus ruber*) weaves through both beds as well.
DESIGN Faith Okuma

TRY A BLEND

▲

Eco-Lawn, a mixture of fescues used here in a front yard in Menlo Park, California, makes a resilient lawn that's as lively looking as a wind-whipped sea. The hummocky texture is most evident when the grass is left gloriously unshorn, but it benefits from shearing twice a year to eliminate seed heads. It's drought-tolerant once established.

TEXTURED CARPETS

If you can't imagine a front yard without some kind of lawn, but you need to get away from the watering, mowing, and fertilizing regime that regular turf requires, you are in luck. There are great alternatives.

GRASSLAND

▶

Native grass, planted as sod, creates a very convincing meadow in this Jackson, Wyoming, front yard. False spirea (*Sorbaria sorbifolia*) and flowering perennials, including Shasta daisies (*Leucanthemum x superbum*), *Salvia nemorosa*, and red valerian (*Centranthus ruber*), add color nearer the house. DESIGN Hershberger Design

GRASS GRID

▶

Slender veldt grass (*Pennisetum spathiolatum*) maintains such a consistent form—1 to 2 feet tall and as wide—that it will retain a graphic pattern. Once established, it needs little irrigation, making it a good choice for planting under oaks, such as the *Quercus agrifolia* in this Arcadia, California, garden. DESIGN Anthony Exter

COOL CREEPER

▶

New Zealand brass button (*Leptinella squalida*), a tough, low-growing perennial that feels pleasantly cushiony underfoot, provides a little breathing space in a Portland front yard. Edging it are crimson flowers of *Persicaria amplexicaulis* 'Firetail'; dark, strappy-leafed *Eucomis comosa* 'Sparkling Burgundy'; and red-tipped *Imperata cylindrica* 'Rubra' grass. DESIGN Debbie Erickson and Nick Erickson

ULTIMATE
WATER-SAVERS

One of the most effective ways to reduce the amount of water
needed to sustain your landscape is to use fewer plants and
more hardscape. If the hardscape is handsome or the way
you have contoured the land is interesting, the results will
not look spare—the plants will stand out by contrast.

PAUSE MAKER
◄◄

Rich, green *Myoporum parvifolium,* a prostrate Australian shrub, edges wide stone slabs interspersed with Mexican beach pebbles leading to the front door of a Santa Barbara, California, home (far left). It grows just 3 to 6 inches tall, provides a dense covering, and is dotted in summer with tiny flowers. Unthirsty shrubs along the driveway (near left) include 'Hidcote' and 'Munstead' English lavender, and prostrate rosemary *(Rosmarinus officinalis* 'Irene'), which spills over the rock wall. Blond grasses fill in. DESIGN Margie Grace

LUNAR DRAMA
►

Contouring the land into undulating waves and then adding a layer of graphite gray decomposed granite gives a familiar combination of desert plants—golden barrel cactus *(Echinocactus grusonii)* and century plant *(Agave americana)*—a fresh, contemporary spin. The blue planter holds *Pedilanthus macrocarpus.* DESIGN Desert Landscape Design

⋛ Design Element ⋛
GLOW

When the sun warms their backs, some plants glow as though lit from within. Ornamental grasses are spectacular examples. Their fine leaves and masses of delicate flowers atop waving stems seem custom-made for back-lighting. Many shrubs also put on great light shows, such as Apache plume (*Fallugia paradoxa*) and smoke tree (*Cotinus*).

Spiny plants also look fabulous when backlit—none more so than jumping cholla (*Opuntia bigelovii*), which is covered with dangerously beautiful silver spines. Prickles don't have to be sinister to look good lighted (think fuzzy but sweet borage blossoms).

Leaves thin enough to be translucent glow like stained glass when the sun is behind them. These include Japanese maples and the giant leaves of canna.

There's a light catcher for every garden style. Take advantage of their energy.

LIGHT CATCHERS

Neat rows of grasses link this San Luis Obispo, California, garden with the vineyards beyond it. In the foreground is *Carex flacca* 'Blue Zinger'; in the middle, *Pennisetum orientale* 'Fairy Tales'; and in back, *Calamagrostis x acutiflora* 'Karl Foerster'.

GRASS + FLOWERS

Grasses make great groundcovers, but they're also great mixers. Thread them through flowering perennials to weave everything together or to add texture to a flowering perennial planted en masse.

FLORAL FANTASY

▼

Deer grass *(Muhlenbergia rigens)* wanders through a hillside of flowering shrubs and perennials in a Santa Cruz, California, garden. The flowers include, up front, Spanish lavender *(Lavandula stoechas)* and wispy, small-flowered *Verbena bonariensis;* in the middle, pink-flowered *Gaura lindheimeri* and rose-purple *Salvia leucantha;* and, at the crest, a purple butterfly bush *(Buddleja davidii).* DESIGN John Greenlee

COUNTRY STYLE

▶

Blue oat grass *(Helictotri-chon sempervirens)* catches the breeze on a slope top in Sunol, California, adding grace and motion to the stiffer textures of succulents *(Sedum telephium)* and Spanish lavender *(Lavandula stoechas).*
DESIGN Jacqueline Authier

MEADOW BLEND

To create the illusion that your garden connects to the wild landscape beyond your property, you have to go a little wild. Plant grasses; they don't have to be the same ones found in the wild, but you should include fine, wispy textures to visually unite the two areas. Then add some flowers, preferably local natives. In this Aspen, Colorado, garden, blue lupine and white Shasta daisies fleck the grasses.

EXPRESSIONISTIC

There is something poetic about ornamental grasses. They can offer effects and instill moods no other class of plant seems to manage. They catch the light, sway in breezes, and create a beautiful haze.

RHYTHM

▼

Bands of tall grasses—slender veldt grass (*Pennisetum spathiolatum*) in the foreground and Atlas fescue (*Festuca mairei*) in the back—border mown *Festuca* 'Bolero Plus' in this Sonoma, California, garden. The visual rhythm against a backdrop of olive trees suggests the ripple of prairie grass in the wind. DESIGN Andrea Cochran

FIREWORKS

◄

The very vertical form of feather reed grass (*Cala-magrostis* x *acutifolia* 'Karl Foerster') makes it look as if it is exploding out of the ground, especially when it is in flower. In this Sonoma, California, garden, it is joined by lavender and olive trees. DESIGN Gary Ratway

VEIL OF MYSTERY

▲

When not in bloom, giant feather grass (*Stipa gigantea*) is an orderly, moderate-size (3-foot) clump. When it flowers, though, it shoots up into a shimmering golden cloud 6 feet tall. In this California North Coast garden, it makes a distant gate appear as a hazy illusion. DESIGN Gary Ratway

CARE TIPS FOR GRASS

Weekly irrigation is sufficient for most established ornamental grasses, and many get by with considerably less water. Don't bother with fertilizing—they look better without it. Forget chemicals; pests and diseases rarely affect grasses. To keep plants from looking ratty, cut them back once a year in late winter or early spring when new growth appears at the base, using hedge shears or power trimmers. Exceptions are evergreen grasses such as *Carex* and blue oat grass, which need renewing every two to three years; comb off dead blades with your (gloved) fingers and cut off dead flowers.

CREATE A MEADOW OR BORROW ONE

You don't need a huge garden to create a meadow—a small grove of trees underplanted with something tall and grassy will do. Another way to go is to borrow a view. If your property looks out on grasslands, planting billowy grasses on the edge of your property that overlooks the view visually unites the two spaces.

GRACEFUL TRANSITION

◀

Two simple grasses, deer grass (*Muhlenbergia rigens*) and a native fescue (*Festuca californica* 'Horse Mountain Green')—plus a sprinkling of simple yarrow (*Achillea millefolium*)—unite a Hollister Ranch, California, garden with the wild rolling hills beyond it.
DESIGN Margie Grace

MINI MEADOW

▼

Two European sedges—*Carex remota* and *Carex divulsa*—flourish under the light shade of a grove of *Liquidambar* trees in a Portola Valley, California, garden.

BEWARE OF INVASIVE GRASSES

Although undeniably beautiful, many grasses need to be used with caution. They produce large amounts of seed, easily dispersed by wind, and can be invasive. If you live close to fragile wilderness, be especially careful. Choose grasses native to your region, or, before planting, check with county extension offices to see if the ornamental grasses you like are potentially invasive in your area. Don't plant jubata grass (*Cortaderia jubata*) or pampas grass (*C. selloana*) in coastal California; giant reed grass (*Arundo donax*) in California or the Southwest; or fountain grass (*Pennisetum setaceum*, also referred to as *Cenchrus setaceus*) in Southern California or the Southwest; or—especially near wildland—Mexican feather grass (*Stipa tenuissima*).

⸘ *Design Element* ⸘
MOTION

A few
live wires on the guest list ensure a great
party. The same thing happens in the
garden.

Include plants that dance in the breeze,
and everything else in the scene seems more
animated. Take clipped hedges—useful and
about as immobile as a room full of furniture.
Add some open-canopied trees overhead
such as olive, whose silvery leaves are
always aquiver, and the hedges no longer
look so stolid. Surround agaves, which are
as striking as statues and nearly as still, with
fine-textured ornamental grasses that billow
and whisper in the slightest puff of air, and
you've brought them out of the gallery and
back into the garden.

Besides animating your garden, wind-
activated plants enliven your mind.

INSPIRED

European meadow sage (*Carex remota*) ripples in the sea breeze on a Malibu, California, bluff-top garden, echoing the Pacific Ocean's waves and swirls beyond. A row of taller grass fringes the meadow. DESIGN Richard Turner

GROUNDCOVERS

The best groundcover plants for various garden situations.

NATIVE NO-MOW LAWNS

These Western grasses create easy-care meadows. See details on page 271.

BLUE GRAMA (Bouteloua gracilis) Grows 1½ to 2 feet tall. Mow at 1½ inches high for a lawn look in low-traffic areas.

BUFFALO GRASS (Buchloe dactyloides) Slow to sprout and fill in, but makes a reasonably dense turf that looks good with little summer water. 'U.C. Verde' has finer texture and is nearly seedless.

FESCUE (Festuca) Red fescue (*F. rubra*) creates a soft, wavy effect when you don't mow it; *F. r.* 'Jughandle' is drought-tolerant. Blue fescue (*F. glauca*) forms clumps.

WALKABLE LAWN SUBSTITUTES

Most of these plants tolerate light foot traffic (except where noted). Grow them in swaths or tuck them between pavers.

CALIFORNIA MEADOW SEDGE (Carex pansa) Forms 6-to-8-inch mats of narrow green leaves. Great between pavers or in small meadows.

DYMONDIA MARGARETAE 'SILVER CARPET' South African native that forms a tight mat, 2 to 3 inches tall and 20 inches wide, of narrow evergreen leaves.

JEWEL MINT OF CORSICA (Mentha requienii) Creeping, mat-forming mint ½ inch tall, dotted with purple flowers. Tiny green leaves release a minty fragrance underfoot.

ROMAN CHAMOMILE (Chamaemelum nobile) Soft, spreading mat of finely cut green leaves on plants 3 to 12 inches tall. Plant 1 foot apart; mow or sheer occasionally to keep tidy.

THYME Mat-forming types include creeping thyme (*Thymus polytrichus brittannicus*), 1 to 3 inches tall spreading to 3 feet wide, with soft gray-green leaves. Similar-sized woolly thyme (*T. serpyllum*) has woolly gray leaves and pink flowers in midsummer. Best between pavers.

LIVING TAPESTRIES

These plants won't take foot traffic; use them for drifts and patches.

BOUGAINVILLEA 'Rosenka' (pink bracts) and 'San Diego Red' (magenta bracts) add vivid color to hillsides in mild-climate gardens.

CALIFORNIA WILD LILAC (Ceanothus) These take little to no summer water once they are established, and need excellent drainage. Point Reyes ceanothus (*C. gloriosus*) grows 1 to 1½ feet tall with dark green leaves and light blue flowers. *C. g. horizontalis* 'Yankee Point', 2 to 3 feet tall with glossy dark green leaves and medium blue flowers, is one of the best ground-covering kinds.

ICE PLANT *Aptenia cordifolia* has stems of apple green leaves and small purplish red blooms in spring and summer; useful in rock gardens. *Delosperma* 'Kelaidis' is cold-tolerant and grows 2 inches high, 1 to 2 feet wide, with pale salmon-pink blooms. *Lampranthus* has large, brilliant blooms; try trailing ice plant (*L. spectabilis*) with gray-green leaves and vivid red-to-purple blooms in winter in mild climates.

JUNIPER Try *Juniperus horizontalis* 'Icee Blue', 4 inches tall, spreading to 8 feet, with silver-blue foliage; blue carpet juniper (*J .h.* 'Wiltonii'), a flat, dense juniper 4 to 6 inches tall, with intense silver-blue foliage; *J. rigida conferta* 'Blue Pacific' with dense blue foliage that's heat-tolerant and grows to 1 foot tall, 8 feet wide; and *J. sabina* 'Calgary Carpet', 6 to 9 inches tall,

10 feet wide, with soft green foliage.

LEMON DWARF WOOLLY YARROW (Achillea tomentosa) Yellow blooms in spring; pretty between pavers and in rock gardens.

MONDO GRASS (Ophiopogon japonicus 'Nana') Dense clumps of deep green leaves grow 6 to 8 inches tall and spread by underground stems. If plants look shabby, mow before spring growth. *O. planiscapus* 'Nigrescens' has black leaves (see page 266).

SEA THRIFT (Armeria maritima) Tufted mounds of narrow green leaves send up little pink ball-shaped blooms over a long season in mild climates.

STONECROP (Sedum) Low mats of shapely, succulent leaves that fit nicely between stones. Gold moss sedum (*S. acre*) has light green leaves and yellow flowers; set plants 1 to 1½ feet apart. *S. album* is a creeping plant 2 to 6 inches tall with green leaves sometimes tinted in red; set plants 1 to 1½ inches apart. *S. spurium* has trailing stems, dark green or bronze leaves, and pink to purple flowers in summer. Most take full sun.

UNDER OAKS

Don't plant within 10 feet of the trunk around large trees.

BEACH STRAWBERRY (Fragaria chiloensis) Low-growing mat, 6 to 12 inches tall, spreads by stolons. Best near the coast; red fruits attract birds.

CREEPING MAHONIA (Mahonia repens) Grows 1 to 3 feet tall and spreads to 10 feet by underground stems. Blue-green, holly-like leaves turn bronze when cold weather arrives. Small flowers are followed by blue berries.

MANZANITA *Arctostaphylos edmundsii* 'Carmel Sur' grows

quickly to 1½ feet tall and 4 to 6 feet wide, with neat gray-green foliage. *A. e.* 'Little Sur' grows 10 inches tall, with green leaves edged in red. Monterey manzanita (*A. hookeri* 'Monterey Carpet') grows to 1 foot tall, 12 feet wide.

SONOMA SAGE (Salvia sonomensis) Native to California's dry foothills, this mat-forming creeper has dull gray leaves and tiny lavender-blue flowers in spring. It grows 12 inches tall and spreads 3 to 4 feet or more.

UNDER REDWOODS

These plants thrive in dry shade.

EVERGREEN HUCKLEBERRY (Vaccinium ovatum) Native to the Pacific Coast, from Santa Barbara north to British Columbia. Grows 2 to 3 feet tall and wide in sun, 8 to 10 feet in shade, with leathery dark green (bronze when new) leaves and whitish flowers followed by black fruits. Takes moderate water.

OREGON GRAPE (Mahonia aquifolium 'Compacta') Grows 2 to 3 feet tall, with coppery green new leaves that turn matte green as they age. Yellow flowers followed by blue berries.

WESTERN SWORD FERN (Polystichum munitum) Most common fern of Western forests; grows 2 to 4 feet tall, with lustrous, dark green fronds. Pretty en masse.

① Black mondo grass (*Ophiopogon planiscapus* 'Nigrescens') with *Pachysandra terminalis* 'Green Sheen'
② *Delosperma* 'Kelaidis'
③ *Dymondia margaretae*
④ Blue fescue (*Festuca glauca*)
⑤ *Sedum oreganum*
⑥ *Juniperus rigida conferta* 'Blue Pacific'
⑦ Golden barrel cactus (*Echinocactus grusonii*, see page 194)

Containers

A FOREST IN POTS

◄

A few containers of the right plants can suggest a whole woodland. At the same time, they can camouflage bare spots or hide areas you don't want people to notice. Here, a dwarf Monterey cypress (*Cupressus macrocarpa* 'Wilma Goldcrest') rises between a lily-of-the-valley shrub (*Pieris japonica*), right, and a *Loropetalum* 'Purple Pixie', whose purple foliage, weeping habit, and compact form make it a container favorite. All prefer part shade. DESIGN Lauren Dunec Hoang and Johanna Silver

TUSCAN ORCHARD

►

Without its underplanting of Irish moss (*Sagina subulata*), this dwarf olive (*Olea europaea* 'Montra') would look like just another tree in a pot. But the moss evokes the shaggy meadow grass under olive groves in Italy, creating a Tuscan villa mood on a West Hollywood patio. Pots of *Echeveria* keep the olive company. DESIGN Scott Shrader

Containers are often treated as ornaments, but they can do so much more. They make ideal focal points. Place a hefty one, planted with a dense evergreen, in the middle of a flower garden to give all those flighty blooms some needed ballast. Watch a bright, glossy pot filled with chartreuse foliage light up a shade garden. Where garden space is limited, container plantings can mimic whole gardens in miniature. Place one big one filled with a bouquet's worth of textures in front of a blank wall, or arrange a handful of pots to create a borderline effect. There is rarely a garden that could not be improved by the addition of a few well-chosen containers.

WOODSY

Leafy greens, whether ferns, grasses, or shrubs, suggest a garden of dappled light shaded by a canopy of tall trees. But you can create that same mood without trees, without shade, or even without dirt, by using the right combination of potted plants. Or, if you really miss the trees, why not plant a grove in miniature?

FOREST FOUNTAIN

▼

Japanese forest grass (*Hakonechloa macra* 'All Gold') is only a few shades lighter than the greenery surrounding it, but the contrast of its dark blue pot makes it seem much lighter. Used this way, one plant brightens up the entire border in this Portland garden. **DESIGN** Mike Darcy

A MOVABLE FEAST

Many perennials look their best in spring, summer, or early fall, then go dormant for winter. Growing them in containers allows you to move them out of sight during their dormant period, then back into a prominent space when they come into bloom. *Euphorbia* 'Blackbird', a cross between *E. amygdaloides* and *E.* x *martinii*, is among the excellent candidates for this use. 'Blackbird' is very vigorous and one of the best *Euphorbia* varieties for containers; its leaves are most colorful in sun.

THREE GRACES

▲

These foliage plants with very different textures bring a border look to a Vancouver, British Columbia, patio. The feathery fern in front (*Polystichum setiferum* 'Herrenhausen') is joined by a weeping *Hakonechloa macra* 'All Gold', at right, and a large, blue-leafed *Hosta fortunei aureomarginata*. The understated pots emphasize the foliage.

DESIGN Todd Holloway

CHAMELEON

◄

With its bright green leaves and dainty appearance, Himalayan honeysuckle (*Leycesteria formosa*) looks like a shade plant, but is happier in bright light. The tiny flowers turn into berries attractive to birds.

MOD

Sleek lines and lava-flow grays create a fresh, contemporary look with all the edgy style of a Hollywood art gallery. Add a spritz of lime or a bit of icy blue to those blacks and charcoals, and the whole tableau comes alive.

ASIAN INFLUENCE

◄

Framed by a Chinese wisteria overhead and a Japanese maple peeking out on the left, two shapely Atlas cedar (Cedrus atlantica) trained on trellises and two fine-leafed golden bamboo fill matte black containers. Together, all these plants give a Glen Ellen, California, garden, its Asian theme.
DESIGN David Fazzio

GRAPHIC

◄

A large bowl of gold Sedum makinoi 'Ogon' and four small square pots of Aeonium arboreum 'Zwartkop' form a pleasing pattern on a concrete table in a Pasadena garden. Throw pillows on the bench behind them reinforce the color scheme.
DESIGN Heather Lenkin

BOLD

Like a sharply uniformed doorman, a solitary striped yucca (*Y. filamentosa* 'Golden Sword') in a tall, charcoal gray pot stands guard at the entrance to a contemporary home. Its companions below, *Festuca glauca* 'Elijah Blue' and green and black *Aeonium,* complement rather than compete with the yucca's bright foliage.

LIVING ART

When the match of plants and pots is spot-on, the result can be more like art than horticulture. Then containers become, in effect, garden sculpture. Place them where they can show off best—whether fronting a bare wall, ornamenting a tabletop, or drawing attention to a garden highlight.

TABLETOP DESERT

◄

Turning a patio table into a work of art, five tiny barrel cactus (*Echinocactus grusonii*), loosely surrounded with clusters of smaller, white-spined thimble cactus (*Mammillaria gracilis*), fill a pale gray ceramic bowl (11 inches in diameter and 4½ inches deep). A mulch of tiny black Aqua Cove pebbles covers the soil around them.
DESIGN Lauren Dunec Hoang

MINI OASIS

►

Tall, sculptural plants in clean, white pots call attention to a strikingly tiled water feature in a Los Angeles garden and give the space the ambience of a desert spa. On the right, a succulent Madagascar palm (*Pachypodium lamerei*) mimics the tropics' best-known trees behind a prickly pear cactus (*Opuntia macrocentra* 'Santa Rita').
DESIGN Mark Tessier

BOAT OF BLUES

►

Succulent rosettes, including mixed varieties of icy blue *Echeveria* and *Grapto-petalum*, fill a low, canoe-shaped container from Bauer Pottery; tiny sedums fill in around them. Lime green *Sedum rupestre* 'Angelina' tucked in at each end will spill over the edges as it grows.
DESIGN Lauren Dunec Hoang

EFFORTLESS
ARTISTRY

Some container vignettes look so natural they appear to have come together almost spontaneously. But before planting, they are often the ones requiring the most thought. The right containers and accessories, and just the right plants for that exact situation, give these vignettes their breezy look.

CASUAL
◄

A variegated *Coprosma* 'Evening Glow', the middle plant in this composition, echoes the colors of the sword-leafed *Phormium* 'Apricot Queen', behind. A fringe of woolly thyme (*Thymus serpyllum*) spills over the edges of the speckled stoneware pot.
DESIGN Lauren Dunec Hoang and Johanna Silver

CALMING
▲

A weathered chunk of teak tree root from Thailand, chosen for its sculptural quality and accented with tillandsia (air plants), sets the tone for this Zen-like garden in Laguna Beach, California. The accompanying containers are large in scale but utterly simple in design, and the plantings they hold are minimal. *Sedum hispanicum* 'Blue Ridge' grows in the bowl in front; *Dianella revoluta* 'Little Rev' in the one behind.
DESIGN Dustin Gimbel

RUSTIC
▲

Haworthia fasciata, with raised white ridges on its pointed leaves, is a good match for the bumpy surface of a volcanic stone bowl. Gray *Echeveria* and bright green *Sedum x rubrotinctum* add a smooth, cooling touch at right. Two rough-surfaced stone spheres, behind, complete the vignette.
DESIGN Ryan Fortini

SINGULAR SENSATIONS

One lone container can make a huge difference in a garden. Placed next to a leafy border, it becomes a focal point that inevitably draws your eye toward the plants beyond. To create the effect you want, go bold. Choose a big pot, perhaps in a bright color, especially for shady spots.

BURST OF BLUE

A large, cobalt blue urn in this California North Coast garden calls attention to the recessed part of the border. The verticality of the ironweed (*Vernonia crinita*) planted in the pot echoes the tall, upright flower stems of white-flowered *Verbascum chaixii*. DESIGN Gary Ratway

POTTED HEDGE

▶

Tall hedges behind mixed borders and short ones in front are expected, but a hedge in a pot smack in the middle is an amusing surprise in this California North Coast garden. The ball of English boxwood (*Buxus sempervirens* 'Green Beauty') is an island of calm in the midst of a flurry of tall *Verbascum* and catmint flower spikes.
DESIGN Gary Ratway

POT OF FIRE

▶

One brilliant plant (*Euphorbia tirucalli* 'Sticks on Fire') in a mustard yellow pot that makes its foliage seem even brighter warms up a low-key grouping of evergreens.

DEVILISHLY DARK

▶

'Black Adder', a big, sprawling, blackish purple *Phormium*, looks twice as dark when planted in a vibrant orange pot. Barely visible around the pot rim beneath its fountainlike leaves is a short, lacy green fringe of *Carex oshimensis* 'Everoro'.

HEAVY METAL

Metal is an unusual but elegant material for planters. Urban gardeners like simple rectangular ones because they are clean and contemporary and corrugated metal ones because they are a bit edgy. Watering troughs look rustic in a country setting, but move them to the city, and they take on an industrial feel. In either situation, if you need a very large container, they are a bargain.

SLEEK

◀

Aluminum planters can appear surprisingly feminine when they are powder-coated, especially when planted in a pastel palette, as in this Los Gatos, California, garden. The agaves are A. *filifera,* and the coral-flowered succulent, *Echeveria* 'Lola.'
DESIGN Jarrod Baumann

GROOVY

▶

Aloe variegata and *Sedum rupestre* 'Angelina' fill this classically shaped container whose corrugated sides give it an industrial edge. The effect is simple yet dramatic.
DESIGN Jarrod Baumann

ARTICHOKE SALAD

▶

Hen and chicks (*Sempervivum*) come in many varieties, as this big bowlful demonstrates. Buy a half-dozen different kinds, arrange them in an attractive pattern in a wide bowl, and you'll have a living sculpture to dress a patio or table for years. If it gets too crowded, pinch out chicks (offsets) and start a second bowl. (For tips on rooting succulents, see page 183.)
DESIGN Todd Holloway

WILD AT HEART

No one wants to be sensible all the time. True, using just one plant per pot and rearranging the pots when you need a change is the easiest, most flexible way to design with containers. But when you want something fresh, throw caution to the wind and plant a tangle. Just make sure that the plants you're combining in a single pot share the same water and exposure needs.

BARELY CONTAINED JUNGLE

▶

The yellow and green stripes of *Canna* 'Pretoria' tower over an exuberant mix of Cuban oregano (*Plectranthus nicodemus*), yellow-flowered *Lantana* 'Honeylove', and a filler of maroon-speckled coleus (*Solenostemon scutellarioides* 'Inky Fingers').

FOLIAGE FESTIVAL

▶

A mass of shrubs mingle in this all-foliage container. *Astelia* 'Silver Shadow' spreads its narrow, blue-green leaves over the red new leaves of *Nandina* 'Obsession' and *Abelia* 'Kaleidoscope', whose leaves blend shades of green, chartreuse, and bronze, and the spiller *Carex oshimensis* 'Everillo'.

POTTED TRIO

◀

Three gorgeous plants vie for attention in a cobalt blue pot—tall, metallic green *Astelia* 'Silver Shadow', dark-violet-flowered *Salvia* 'Amistad', and weeping chartreuse *Carex oshimensis* 'Everillo'.

KEEP
IT SIMPLE

One plant per pot is the easiest way to design containers. Select plants that have interesting foliage and/or shapes and don't grow too fast, then give each its own container. Arrange the pots until you are pleased, and you're done. If one plant fails, replace it with something else, or bring in another pot from elsewhere in the garden. No need to start over. If you prefer more complex plantings, try the thriller/filler/spiller approach (far right). It never fails.

ASYMMETRICAL ARRANGEMENT

◄

When putting together container vignettes, it is best to use an odd number. This composition, with four pots, appears to break the rule. But because the fifth pot in the back matches two others up front on this patio, it looks as if it's part of the vignette. The upright plant in the blue pot holds *Yucca recurvifolia*. To the right is 'Purple Queen' bougainvillea. The succulent in front is *Graptopetalum paraguayense*. The tree in the fifth pot is a kumquat.

AMBER TRIO

►

Successful container vignettes usually employ repetition in some form. Here, the unifying factor is the pots. They are the same shape, nearly the same size, and in a close range of colors. The tall plant at right is *Euphorbia tirucalli,* the red plant in back is *E. t.* 'Sticks on Fire', and the plant at left is a variegated agave.
DESIGN Joshua Stenzel

FOLLOW A FORMULA

To create a great container planting, all you have to do is remember three words: *thriller, filler, spiller*. The thriller is the tallest plant in a composition; put it in the center or toward the back of the container. The filler is the lower, fluffier plant that grows around it, and the spiller tumbles over the pot's rim. Here, the thriller is apricot-colored *Phormium* 'Maori Queen'; the filler, icy blue *Senecio mandraliscae*; and the spiller, *Calibrachoa* 'Double Orange'. Having a striking pot like this swimming pool blue one enhances the planting. DESIGN Johanna Silver

GARDENS IN POTS

Planting containers well can be a little like being a set designer. Picking a handful of plants that will live together in a single pot is just the beginning. The plants you choose also have to complement the color, texture, and shape of the pot you've selected, and must share the same needs for water and location (whether sun or shade). The pot should be just right for the setting you have in mind.

MEDITERRANEAN-CLIMATE MEDLEY

◄

Ozothamnus 'Sussex Silver', a tall, wispy New Zealand shrub, shimmers against a rusty metal wall in a pot that looks dyed to match. Its companions underfoot are, left to right, green *Senecio vitalis*, rose-tinged *Echeveria gibbiflora,* and silvery green pig's ear (*Cotyledon orbiculata oblonga*). Fluffy green *Asparagus retrofractus*, a South African native, adds cool contrast at right.
DESIGN Daniel Nolan

LIVING BOUQUET

▲

The velvety, tannish leaves of this felt plant (*Kalanchoe beharensis*) are so well suited to the big, rough-textured clay pot they are planted in that the two almost seem one. Light green *Aeonium* 'Kiwi' fills in below, picking up the sea foam green of the new growth of the *K. beharensis*. Both are frost-tender.
DESIGN Tish Treherne

WOODLAND ARRAY

▲

Huckleberry (*Vaccinium ovatum*), the tallest plant in this pot on a Seattle patio, grows up to 10 feet tall in the wild but does well in containers too. Here, it is accompanied by *Leucothoe fontanesiana* and two spillers—wire vine (*Muehlenbeckia complexa*) trailing out the front and *Carex hachijoensis* 'Evergold' arching like wings over the sides. DESIGN Kenneth Philp

SPACE MAKERS

Every garden has a few spaces that are too small or too skinny, or have too much paving to be planted. Entries, front and back, are good examples. To keep them from looking conspicuously empty, use a cluster of containers. Just a few or even one lushly planted one—to turn these blank canvases into landscapes.

SUCCULENT SHOWCASE
◄

Plump succulents cluster in front of corrugated metal fencing in Bainbridge Island, Washington. Purple *Aeonium arboreum* 'Zwartkop', along with a little Mexican feather grass (*Stipa tenuissima*), fills the largest pot. A variegated agave (*A. parryi patonii* 'Variegata') grows in the speckled pot at right, while two varieties of *Echeveria* share the third pot. A bouquet of succulents, tucked into the ground up front, softens and anchors the vignette.
DESIGN Tish Treherne

AUSSIE WELCOME
►

A big bronze pot filled with Australian shrubs greets guests at the entrance to this Los Angeles home. The tall one is willow wattle (*Acacia iteaphylla*), and the spiller is woolly bush (*Adenanthos drummondii*). Deep purple *Aeonium arboreum* 'Zwartkop' adds both contrasting color and texture.
DESIGN Sasha Tarnopolsky

CONIFER CORRAL
◄

A variety of conifers, all in pots, creates textural interest next to a wood fence in a Portland garden. The collection includes, left to right, two cedars—the very vertical *Chamaecyparis lawsoniana* 'Treasure Island' and its shorter neighbor, *C. l.* 'Duncanii'—a hemlock (*Tsuga canadensis* 'Jacqueline Verkade'); and an umbrella pine (*Sciadopitys verticillata* 'Joe Kozey') tucked behind a honeysuckle (*Lonicera* 'Lemon Beauty'). *Sedum* 'Palmeri' fills the square pot. A trumpet vine (*Campsis* x 'Mme Galen') adds a shot of color along the fence.
DESIGN Susan LaTourette

SPOT OF RED

▲

Echeveria x *imbricata* in a bright red bowl draws attention to a palm trunk repurposed as a side table in a Los Angeles garden. The flash of color also directs the eye to the jungle of plants, including a bronze-leafed *Phormium*, behind, and spiky *Aloe arborescens* 'Variegata', in front. DESIGN Joseph Marek

TABLE DRESSING

On occasion, the main role of a container is to decorate a patio or table for summer gatherings outdoors. It is there to please the eye, amuse the mind, add a spark of color, or reflect the personality of the garden's owner. Sometimes that is enough.

SUN AND SEA

▲

Despite the sunny yellow pot they are
housed in, these two succulents, red-
tinged *Crassula capitella* 'Campfire'
and green *Crassula congesta,* evoke
the ocean's kelp beds, creating an
entertaining coffee-table centerpiece.
DESIGN Annette Gutierrez

COLLECTIBLES

▲

Containers don't have to match one
another to create a pretty vignette.
Mixed sizes, shapes, and colors can
work well together as long as the plants
in them are related. In this Los Angeles
garden, small succulents including a
hen and chicks fill a long narrow bowl
on a buffet table; *Aeonium* 'Sunburst'
shares space with sedum in a tall red
pot; a speckled *Mangave* cools off in
an ice blue pot; and living stones
(*Lithops*) fill a small charcoal bowl.
DESIGN Annette Gutierrez

ROUGHLY REFINED
▲

The artistically weathered surfaces of three similar but not identical pots perfectly complement the tough customers they hold. In front is a small variegated agave surrounded by tiny sedums. To its left is coppery-leafed *Kalanchoe orgyalis* with hen and chicks. A blue-green *Echeveria* grows in the large pot. DESIGN Joshua Stenzel

WHITE ON WHITE
▲

A single container, planted simply, is often all you need for big impact. In this beachy vignette, beside a front entry in Newport Beach, California, apple green "dinner plate" *Aeonium urbicum* fills a textured white stone urn. Matching lanterns anchor the arrangement. DESIGN Molly Wood

THEATRICAL TABLEAU
▶

Five glossy black pots, each holding one striking plant, are a great starting point. The plants, left to right: *Acacia iteaphylla;* the bromeliad *Vriesea philippo coburgii;* cascading mistletoe cactus (*Rhipsalis baccifera*); *Euphorbia tirucalli,* in the tallest pot; and *Yucca aloifolia* 'Purpurea'. But two additional pots are very different in texture and shape—one planted in agaves, the other in *Sempervivum*—and elevate the arrangement to theater. DESIGN Joshua Stenzel

ARRANGING CONTAINERS

Although putting together a pleasing composition of containers is partially an intuitive process, here are some guidelines to help you do it better. Unless you prefer a formal, symmetrical design, use an odd rather than even number of pots. You can plant something different in each container, but decide on a unifying theme for the ones you plan to show off together. The pots could all be the same color, or same material, or same shape, for instance. Or, if you have a collection of diverse containers, keep the plants the same—green and gray *Santolina*, for instance, or a selection of various *Echeveria*.

TIPS from a PRO

In his work as a designer at Flora Grubb Nursery in San Francisco, **JOSHUA STENZEL** often mixes quirky drought-tolerant plants from Australia and the South-west. Here's how he gets his dazzling results.

COLOR COORDINATE

Start with a plant or pot you love and let it lead the design. A glazed container the color of burnt sugar, for example, suggests plants with bronze or caramel-and-olive-hued foliage, such as some *Coprosma*.

GO FOR BOLD

Skip the dainty little pots and go for big and bold. Repeat strong colors.

INCLUDE LACE

"I almost always include something lacy, something hanging, something architectural," he says.

THROW IN A SURPRISE

It could be *Sempervivums* dripping their pups out of a low pot.

PURPOSEFUL POTS

Containers are more than decorative. They can be problem-solvers too. Use them to disguise areas you don't want people to notice—pool equipment, for instance, or the worn status of an old fence. Or use them to define the edges of an outdoor room or to create the look of a border on a patio.

CITRUS CORNER
▶

Pots in mouthwatering colors—tangerine, lime, and watermelon-rind green—massed together under the shelter of a bougainvillea vine and a citrus tree, create a solo retreat in a Hollywood garden. The tall, deep, green pot contains a big *Agave attenuata* and *Aeonium;* the lime pot, another *Aeonium;* and the tangerine pot, *Graptoveria* 'Fred Ives'. *Lithops* grows in the hollowed-out stone in front, next to a silver-pink *Echeveria* 'Afterglow'. DESIGN Annette Gutierrez

OUTDOOR PARLOR
◀

Four large identical pots planted with 'Sum and Substance' hostas give a front-yard seating area in a Portland garden a feeling of enclosure during the warm season. This cozy space used to be a lawn struggling under too shady conditions. DESIGN JJ DeSousa

FLOWER-BED FIREWORKS
▶

Cordyline 'Design-a-Line Burgundy' sends out arching red leaves that appear to burst like fireworks above a bed of cool blue 'Chef's Choice' rosemary, left, and *Astelia* 'Silver Sword', right. Ringed with silvery succulent rosettes, the cordyline grows in a deep container that is partially sunk into the ground so it can be easily swapped out for a different accent plant. DESIGN Janet Sluis

CONTAINER PLANTS

From foliage to flowers, here are showy, compact choices.
For immediate effect, start with 1- or 5-gallon nursery plants.

COMPACT TREES

*These evergreens look good
in all seasons.*

KUMQUAT Plants tend toward
small. Especially on dwarfing
rootstocks, they reach only 3 to
6 feet tall. Pretty in winter when
dressed with orange fruits.

**'LITTLE OLLIE' OLIVE (Olea
europaea)** Grows 6 to 8 feet tall
and wide with densely packed
silvery green foliage.

**PEPPERMINT TREE (Agonis
flexuosa 'Jervis Bay Afterdark')**
One of the best small trees for
California gardens where
temperatures stay above 27°.
Eventually reaches 18 feet tall,
but grows slowly, so start when
young in a large container. The
feathery burgundy foliage is
pretty with burgundy *Heuchera*
'Crimson Curls' and *Grevellia*
'Fanfare', whose leaves turn
coppery hues with age.

SMALL SHRUBS

*Grow these for their foliage
or flowers.*

BOXWOOD Best for pots include
Buxus microphylla 'Compacta',
which grows just 1 foot tall and
wide and has yellowish new
leaves (green when mature), and
B. microphylla 'Golden Triumph',
which rarely grows beyond
3 feet tall in 10 years and has
green leaves edged in yellow.

COPROSMA HYBRIDS Shiny
leaves come in many gorgeous
colors. 'Tequila Sunrise' blends
yellow, emerald green, and deep
orange in its glossy leaves.
'Evening Glow' has green and
gold leaves that turn orange-red
in fall. For drama, try smoldering
'Roy's Red' or 'Karo Red'.

**DWARF POMEGRANATE (Punica
granatum 'Nana')** Grows to 2 to
3 feet tall, 4 to 5 feet wide. Orange-
red flowers are followed by
small, dry red fruit.

GARDEN HYDRANGEA Compact
types such as 'Pink Elf' and
'Endless Summer' thrive in
containers.

LAVENDER Best kinds for pots
include *Lavandula angustifolia*
'Blue Cushion', 1½ to 2 feet tall
with bright violet-blue flowers;
foot-tall *L. a.* 'Lavender Lady',
with gray-green leaves and short
spikes of lavender-blue flowers;
and *L. a.* 'Compacta', 1½ feet
tall with gray-green foliage and
light lavender flowers.

LOROPETALUM 'PURPLE PIXIE'
Weeping groundcover with deep
burgundy-chocolate leaves.
Pretty in a big glazed pot of
chocolate brown.

**PIERIS JAPONICA 'MOUNTAIN
SNOW'** More heat-tolerant than
standard *P. japonica*. Grows
3 to 4 feet tall and has bronze-
colored new foliage and hanging
clusters of tiny, ivory-white spring
blooms.

**SHRIMP PLANT (Justicia brande-
geeana)** Mild-climate evergreen
from Mexico. Grows 3 to 4 feet
tall with pink to orange blooms
from spring to fall.

GRASSES, PLUS

Fab foliage carries the show.

**BLACK MONDO GRASS (Ophio-
pogon planiscapus 'Nigrescens')**
Narrow leaves are black. For
a spooky, spiderlike Halloween
show on the front porch, plant it
in a 12-inch-wide black-glazed
pot to display among pumpkins.

CAREX *C. testacea* has thin
leaves with orange highlights.
C. oshimensis 'Everillo' has
glossy, lime green leaves that
spill gracefully over pot rims.

CORDYLINE 'DESIGN-A-LINE'
Cascading, grasslike plant with
bronze-red foliage. Easy and
water-wise, it holds its color
throughout the year.

OZOTHAMNUS ROSMARINIFOLIUS
Mild-climate Australian native
with dense, narrow, dark green
leaves and closely packed red
buds in summer. Grows 6 to
10 feet tall, but can live for a
few years in large pots.

PHORMIUM 'Yellow Wave' grows
4 to 5 feet tall and has chartreuse
leaves with lime green margins.
Pretty in a yellow pot. 'Black
Adder' grows slowly to 3 to
4 feet tall; deep burgundy leaves
are sword-shaped, each with a
beautiful arching habit. 'Maori
Sunrise', 3 feet tall, 4 to 5 feet
wide, has apricot to pink leaves
striped in green.

**SEA OATS (Chasmanthium lati-
folium)** Perennial grass that forms
clumps of broad, bamboo-like
leaves and green seed heads
atop stems 2 to 5 feet tall. Turns
coppery hues in fall.

PERENNIALS

*Move these plants to center
stage when in bloom.*

CATMINT (Nepeta x faassenii)
Forms a soft, silvery gray-green
mound, to 1 foot tall, of small,
gray-green leaves. Delicate
clusters of small, violet-blue
flowers in spring. Pretty as a
fringe for *Salvia coccinea*
'Brenthurst', which has vivid
salmon blooms.

CHRYSANTHEMUM Hard to beat
for blooms in late summer to fall.
Small-flowered garden mums
come in many pretty colors, from
rust, to red and pink, to yellow.
Cut the plants back to just above
new growth each winter. Plants
can live for years in containers.

CORAL BELLS (Heuchera) Compact, mounding, evergreen plants
prized for their shapely leaves in
a big range of colors, from lime
and caramel to chocolate brown
flecked with pink. Most send up
spikes of tiny pink or red flowers
in spring.

DAHLIA Beautiful summer blooms
in a variety of shapes and colors;
best for pots are small-flowered
bush varieties. Plant corms, one
per 14-inch-diameter pot, after
weather warms in spring. Once
bloom is through, stop watering
plants and move pots to a dry,
protected spot such as a garden
shed or garage until spring.

**KANGAROO PAW (Anigozanthos
hybrids)** Clumping perennials
from Australia with grasslike
foliage. Best for containers are
compact types in the Bush Gems
series. 'Bush Gold' has lemon
yellow blooms above lime green
leaves; 'Bush Ranger' has red
blooms; and 'Bush Baby' flowers
blend red, orange, and yellow.
All stay below 3 feet tall.

SAGE Smallest species are best.
Try *Salvia coccinea* 'Brenthurst',
with salmon blooms, or 'Lady-
in-Red', with bright red blooms.
Both grow 2 to 3 feet tall. Plants
overwinter in mild climates
(although weedy in Hawaii).
Freshen them in early spring by
cutting back to new growth.

**SCENTED GERANIUMS (Pelar-
gonium)** Most grow 1 to 3 feet
tall, with showy, scented foliage
that trumps the small flowers.
Try *P. crispum* for lemon
fragrance, lime geranium
(*P.* 'Nervosum'), or apple-
scented *P. odoratissimum*.

SUCCULENTS

Many; see pages 194–195.

❶ *Coprosma* 'Tequila Sunrise'
❷ *Phormium* 'Jester', in back,
with X *Graptosedum*
❸ *Carex testacea*
❹ *Heuchera* in a range of
colors
❺ Catmint (*Nepeta x faassenii*)
❻ *Loropetalum* 'Purple Pixie'
❼ Garden hydrangea
(*H. macrophylla* 'Endless
Summer')
❽ Kangaroo paw
(*Anigozanthos*)
❾ Chrysanthemum

Tips

Spring

Temperatures are warming, plants are starting to grow, and blooms are unfurling. It's time to plant, feed, water, and mulch.

◀ Cranesbill (*Erodium reichardii*), a dainty-looking but tough plant from the Mediterranean region, forms a dense tuft of foliage 3 to 6 inches tall.

SOFTEN A PATH

To get groundcovers between pavers off to a great start, you need good soil. Before nestling the pavers, put down at least 6 inches of high-quality planting mix—not just in the areas where you anticipate planting, but under the whole path. That way, you can keep altering the placement of pavers and plants until you're satisfied. Once you plant, you'll encourage roots to spread quickly.

Where foot traffic is heavy, create narrow gaps between pavers; where it is more occasional, leave up to 4 inches between stones for planting. Choose low-growing groundcovers such as *Dymondia margaretae* for well-used areas; sprawlers, such as thyme and chamomile, for side paths. The intersections where three or more stones meet are good places to drop in *Carex*, *Festuca*, or other, taller accent plants.

Plant as densely as you can. Buy groundcovers in flats, cut them apart into small squares, and plant the plugs as close as 6 inches apart. The quicker the gaps fill in, the less time you'll need to spend pulling up weeds. Once the plants have filled in, an hour a month is about all you need to maintain a path about 30 feet long and 5 feet wide.

PLANT A BEE BAR

1 Select a diverse array of bee-friendly flowers, such as coral bells (*Heuchera*) and borage, pictured at right, to attract pollinators. Other good choices: asters, bee balm (*Monarda*), sweet alyssum, and sunflowers. Include early-, mid-, and late-season bloomers to keep a steady supply of nectar.

2 Set aside some bare patches of soil where solitary native bees can build their nests. Don't cover them with mulch. And avoid using pesticides.

SMART TIP

DIVIDE PLANTS

Dig and divide big, overgrown perennials, then replant the divisions. The more material you already have, the less you need to buy.

ESSENTIALS

PRUNE After spring-flowering shrubs and vines bloom, remove dead, diseased, or injured branches. Pinch faded flower trusses from rhododendrons and azaleas. In mountain areas, prune winter-dormant trees, roses, and vines.

WATER Deep-water permanent non-native plants every 7 to 10 days. In a desert climate, give drip-irrigated plants at least one deep watering to leach accumulated salts from root zones.

FEED After blooms fade, apply high-nitrogen fertilizer to spring-flowering shrubs. When active growth starts, also feed other shrubs, trees, perennials, and vines with a high-nitrogen fertilizer such as 20-10-5. Feed roses after each bloom cycle. Every 2 to 3 weeks, give container plants a dose of a half-strength liquid fertilizer, or apply a granular, controlled-release fertilizer.

MULCH Cover the bare ground around each plant with a 3-inch layer of mulch to help conserve soil moisture, suppress weeds, and keep the soil cooler. Use organic types such as bark chips, shredded bark, or compost that will improve the soil as they break down.

Grow a Better Grass

Want a spot of lawn but not the big water bill? In years of normal rainfall, the grasses here can live without extra irrigation in their native ranges, and they need mowing just once or twice a year. Plant from plugs (hair grass is pictured). Prep the soil before planting by adding a 3-inch layer of clean, weed-free topsoil; rake smooth.

DESERT Fine fescue, spring-planted buffalo grass, blue grama.

NORTHERN CALIFORNIA, NORTHWEST Fine fescue, hair grass (*Deschampsia*).

SOUTHERN CALIFORNIA Fine fescue or spring planted 'UC Verde' buffalo grass (along coast).

ROCKY MOUNTAIN Buffalo grass or blue grama below 6,500 feet; fine fescue above.

◄ A flat of plugs is enough to cover 30 square feet. Remove plugs from their sleeves, water well, then plant 8 inches apart.

▼ This grass took a year to fill in, with 5-minute waterings twice a week (pull weeds until it fills in).

GROW A BUFFET FOR BUTTERFLIES

Set out nectar-rich flowering plants, and monarchs and swallowtails will drop by, bringing beauty and motion to the garden. Add some larval plants for their caterpillar offspring, and they'll stick around to mate and lay eggs. Butterfly weed (*Asclepias tuberosa*) attracts both larvae and adults. Other nectar producers: aster (*A. cordifolius*, *A. x frikartii*, and *A. x f.* 'Mönch'); black-eyed Susan; coneflower; coreopsis; *Gaillardia*; lantana (pictured); and yarrow (*Achillea*).

Summer

Summer Time to relax and enjoy your garden. It's also the season for clipping spent blooms, planting water-wise containers, refreshing bare spots, and planning ahead.

BEACH IN A BOWL

If you yearn for the beach but live miles inland, try this. Fill a low bowl with cactus mix and plant small succulents. Spritz the soil with water; mulch using washed sand. Finish with shells or bits of

DITCH THE LAWN

If you're looking to replace turf in fall with water-wise plants, here are five ways to get rid of it by summer's end.

DRY IT OUT. Stop watering, and fine, short-rooted grass probably won't survive the summer. (Fleshy or deep-rooted grasses will likely resprout in the rainy season.)

DIG IT UP. Use a sharp flat-edge shovel to dig up the turf, piece by piece. Dig deep enough to sever grass roots. Turn each piece over to compost in place, or move the turf to the compost pile.

SMOTHER IT. Put a 4-to-6-inch layer of mulch over fine, short-rooted grass, and the turf will compost beneath it. Keep the mulch moist until the grass is dead, in 4 to 6 weeks. You can then plant directly into the mulch.

SOLARIZE IT. In the heat of summer, mow the grass short, water well, then cover with 1-to-4-mil-thick clear plastic. Spread the plastic beyond the lawn's perimeter and weigh down the edges with bricks or rocks. Then let the sun cook it for 6 to 8 weeks in cool climates, 4 to 6 weeks in warm climates, and 4 weeks in hottest climates. Remove the plastic.

SHRINK IT. Dig and turn under all but a 3-foot-wide ribbon of grass (enough to cool bare feet), then amend the soil on either side and plant unthirsty perennials.

driftwood. Start with an *Echeveria* rosette, then add smaller leafed kinds like the ones tucked in below.

MEADOW GRASSES 101

Meadows are a lot more entertaining than turf. They shiver in breezes, capture the light, provide homes for ground-nesting birds, and make country landscapes feel right at home. But unless you're lucky enough to live on the edge of a natural, knee-high meadow like the one pictured, outside a beach house on Savary Island, British Columbia, you'll need to plant one.

The three grasses below, all clumping, make great garden choices for sunny spots that get little irrigation; all need soil with good drainage. Tuck in some lavender, pineleaf penstemon, or other dry-climate plants for color, or a smattering of boulders to enhance the dry theme.

Indian rice grass (*Oryzopsis hymenoides*) Green leaves turn brown in summer. Grows 1 to 2 feet tall.

Big bluestem (*Andropogon gerardii*) Blue-green leaves become coppery in fall. Grows 3 to 5 feet tall.

Little bluestem (*Schizachyrium scoparium*) Foliage is bluish in summer, light brown to reddish in fall. Grows 2 to 4 feet tall.

Lime Spritzers

Brighten beds and borders by tucking in chartreuse foliage plants. Here are three favorites.

1 ***Sedum rupestre* 'Angelina'** A fluffy groundcover with small yellow blooms in summer. Sun.

2 **'Lemon Fizz' santolina** A sizzling chartreuse that would be perfect for a bolt of silk. The every-which-way foliage of this shrub is fun too. Sun.

3 **'Lime Rickey' coral bells (*Heuchera*)** Ruffled leaves of this evergreen perennial emerge chartreuse, then age to lime green. Part shade.

ESSENTIALS

WATER Deeply irrigate plants that need it in early morning. If drought persists, water trees with a root irrigator or soaker hoses to moisten the soil 18 to 24 inches deep within the dripline. Do not water established native plants; many are prone to disease when the soil around them is kept wet in summer.

FEED Container plants should be fed twice a month with half-strength liquid fertilizer.

MULCH Spread a 3-inch layer of organic mulch such as ground bark or pine needles around landscape plants to conserve moisture and reduce weeds.

PRUNE Cut off spent blooms on perennials such as coreopsis, cosmos, dahlias, and gloriosa daisies to keep blooms coming.

COMPOST Mix garden waste with grass clippings and mature compost or compost starter to activate a new pile.

SHOP Buy summer-blooming perennials at nurseries now, but wait until cooler fall days to plant. Easy drought-tolerant choices include aster, coneflower, coreopsis, *Gaillardia*, gloriosa daisy, and yarrow. In mildest climates, add *Gazania*, *Osteospermum*, *Salvia leucantha*, and sea lavender.

Fall

In mild winter climates, the time is right to plant trees, shrubs, and perennials; to cut back spent perennials; and to clean up and compost garden debris.

Here are 10 garden-friendly wildflowers.

1. Blackfoot daisy (*Melampodium leucanthum*)
2. California poppy (*Eschscholzia californica*)
3. Baby blue eyes (*Nemophila menziesii*)
4. Perennial blue flax (*Linum perenne*)
5. California desert bluebells (*Phacelia campanularia*)
6. Desert marigold (*Baileya multiradiata*)
7. Farewell-to-spring (*Clarkia amoena*)
8. Lupine (*Lupinus succulentus*)
9. Tidytips (*Layia platyglossa*)
10. Wine cups (*Callirhoe involucrata*)

WILDFLOWERS

You don't need a road trip to find wildflowers—they'll grow in garden beds and even in containers, if you choose the right ones. Buy a seed mix designed for your climate; an ounce of seed can cover 100 square feet. Broadcast the seeds over weed-free soil in a sunny spot, following package instructions. Lightly rake the soil to cover the seeds. And pray for rain!

HOT SHRUBS

Shrubs are getting prettier all the time, and they're among the easiest plants to grow. These are especially striking.

1 **Barberry (*Berberis thunbergii* 'Sunjoy Tangelo')** An attractive accent for grasses, it forms a neat mound of bright orange foliage, often with a lime green edging. Takes drought; prefers well-drained soil. Grows 4 to 5 feet tall. Sun.

2 **'Goldflame' spirea (*Spiraea japonica* 'Goldflame')** A dense, mounding shrub, 3 to 4 feet tall, with bronze-tinged new foliage that matures to soft yellow-green. Deciduous. Leaves turn coppery orange in fall. Sun.

3 **Ninebark (*Physocarpus opulifolius* 'Coppertina')** Copper-flushed spring foliage turns rich burgundy red in summer. Peeling bark adds interest in winter; small pinkish white flower clusters in spring. Grows 6 to 8 feet tall. Sun or shade.

ESSENTIALS

PLANT Set out trees and shrubs in berry or fall colors, and blooming perennials such as aster and *Helianthus* 'Lemon Queen'. In mountain states, do this no later than 6 weeks before the ground freezes.

PROTECT PLANTS Around midmonth in the coldest zones, reduce water to woody plants to encourage fall dormancy. Don't feed again until next year.

DIG DAHLIAS Give them a few days to dry, then store the tubers in wooden boxes filled with dry peat moss in a cool, dry place.

DIVIDE PERENNIALS Dig and pull apart overcrowded, clumping, warm-season types such as Shasta daisy; replant divisions. In cold winter areas, do this early.

Soil Amendments—How Much to Buy

A small (half-ton) pickup truck holds about 1 cubic yard of compost (five wheelbarrow loads). Landscape-supply companies will deliver bulk orders; nurseries sell bagged compost. Here's how much you need to add a 2-, 3-, or 4-inch layer of soil amendment.

YARD SIZE	2" AMENDMENT	3" AMENDMENT	4" AMENDMENT
100 sq. ft.	⅔ cubic yd.	1 cubic yd.	1¼ cubic yds.
250 sq. ft.	1⅔ cubic yds.	2½ cubic yds.	3¼ cubic yds.
500 sq. ft.	3¼ cubic yds.	4⅔ cubic yds.	6¼ cubic yds.
1,000 sq. ft.	6½ cubic yds.	9¼ cubic yds.	12½ cubic yds.

LEAF TRICK

When the leaves fall into finely textured ground-covers, they're difficult to get out. Rake them, and you can pull up the groundcover; leave them where they fall, and they can turn into a soggy mess that smothers the plants below. What to do? At first sign of leaf drop, lay bird netting over the groundcover. Once the tree is bare, pull up the netting, and most of the leaves with it. Compost them.

SMART TIP

BUY SMALL

Plants in 4-inch pots cost less than those in 1-gallon cans, and they can establish just as fast.

Winter

It's time to prune roses, evergreens, deciduous trees, and shrubs; to plant winter bloomers and bare-root shrubs; and to savor the season outdoors.

SMART TIP

PROTECT PLANTS

In cold winter areas, knock snow off the branches of shrubs and trees before it breaks or disfigures them.

STYLISH COMBO

Bloodtwig dogwood (*Cornus sanguinea* 'Midwinter Fire') is striking enough in winter when its leafless branches show their color. But plant a ruff of black mondo grass (*Ophiopogon planiscapus* 'Nigrescens') around it, and you can turn a quiet corner into living art.

COMPACT CONIFERS

Much of the West is prime country for conifers, and winter is the season to fully appreciate just how much they contribute to the landscape. The best kinds for most suburban and city gardens, though, are compact types such as the dwarf mugo pine (*Pinus mugo* 'Mitch Mini'), pictured above in a Northwest garden; it grows slowly, less than a foot in 10 years. Other low growers, in shades of blue-green to gold, include *Chamaecyparis obtusa* 'Nana Lutea'; steel blue *Abies lasiocarpa* 'Glauca Compacta'; *Pinus strobus* 'Blue Shag'; and golden *Thuja occidentalis* 'Rheingold'. Look for plants at nurseries in 1- and 5-gallon cans.

FROSTY FLOWERS

Winter may be the most dramatic season for many ornamental grasses and flowering perennials—if you don't cut them back for winter. Like icing on a cake, frost cloaks the flower stems of these three plants, making them glisten in morning light (left to right): giant feather grass (*Stipa gigantea*); sea holly (*Eryngium*); and Lady's-Mantle (*Alchemilla mollis*).

◄ WOODLAND SPRITES

Looking for winter color to tuck in along paths? Try hardy cyclamen, which unfurl tiny winged blooms in shades of pink that appear to perch atop stems like butterflies. Plant them in dry shade, in rich, well-drained soil, with the tops of the round tubers above the soil.

Water-thrifty Roses

Many roses prefer regular watering, but a number of heirloom and old species roses thrive on the coast and in inland valleys with little or no water during summer. They include 'Albertine', a rambler with copper apricot-pink blooms; 'Belle Portugaise' (pale pink); 'Cl. Cécile Brünner' (pink); Lady Banks' (*Rosa banksiae* 'Lutea'), pictured; 'Paul Ricault' (deep pink); *R. rugosa* 'Alba' (white) and 'Rubra' (bright pink); and 'Silver Moon' (white).

ESSENTIALS

EVERGREENS Prune evergreens to shape plants (as needed). Use prunings of evergreen magnolia, juniper, pine, fir, cedar, and redwood for holiday wreaths and swags.

ROSES Cut back hybrid tea roses by about a third; leave the most vigorous three to five canes, forming a vase shape. Remove diseased and injured canes along the way. Prune landscape roses to shape.

SHRUBS Prune deciduous types such as fairy duster and hydrangea, as well as deciduous ornamentals such as forsythia and quince, after they bloom.

GRASSES In late winter, cut back clumping ornamental grasses to just above new growth emerging from the base. Fresh blades will soon take over.

EASY ACCENTS

For splashes of summer color in sunny borders, plus blooms for bouquets, tuck some dahlias into the ground between shrubs and grasses. Dig out and store the tubers for winter.

Steps to Grow By

Easy-care gardening has a two-fold goal:
to reduce maintenance time and to ensure that the time
you do spend on chores is as pleasurable as possible.
Here's how to refresh a tired garden corner
or to start a garden from scratch.

BEFORE YOU START

CONSIDER CLIMATE The garden you plan should be in harmony with your local climate. Consider water, soil, wind, and light conditions, rainfall patterns, and cloud or fog cover.

Throughout the West, aridity and recurring droughts are major concerns; choose plants with low water needs.

Wooded foothills offer ideal growing conditions for many shrubs and trees, but wildfires are a regular threat; select fire-resistant plants as part of your defensive strategy.

Above 8,000 feet, the growing season is short; frost and snow are possible any month of the year. Winters are extremely cold, but a snow cover can help protect plants. Cool summers favor many perennials.

ANALYZE YOUR SITE Choose plants that appeal to you and suit your climate and site; plant them where they'll grow best. East and north sides of the house are good locations for plants that like some shade, especially later in the day. Warmer southern exposures and protected areas are good spots for slightly tender plants.

AT THE NURSERY

BUY THE BEST Look for plants that have healthy foliage and no roots creeping out of the nursery container's bottom drain holes (which means the plants are probably rootbound).

SMALL IS SMARTER Buy plants in 4-inch nursery pots; they are less expensive (usually under $5), are easier to handle, and will catch up to the larger ones with winter rains. Smaller plants are your best bet if you need multiples to fill out a bed. Gallon-size plants, on the other hand, start around $10 each but can provide instant effects.

CHECK PLANT TAGS Find out how big the plants will grow, and whether they need sun or shade. Then choose plants that will thrive in the spot you have in mind for them. "Full sun" means you should plant in a spot that gets at least 6 hours of sun a day.

CONSIDER COMPOST Unless you have your own compost pile or perfect garden soil that drains well, buy bagged compost to add to the soil before planting annuals, edibles, and many ornamentals (trees and native plants generally do not need added compost). It's often sold at nurseries in 1- and 2-cubic-foot bags and in bulk at garden suppliers. Avoid bagged compost that looks as though it has been piled and stored in hot sun for months—it won't do much for your soil.

IN YOUR GARDEN

IMPROVE YOUR SOIL Dig up the existing garden soil to a depth of about 10 inches, breaking up clods and removing stones as you go. Then, unless you're planting trees or natives, spread 4 to 6 inches of compost over the area and dig it in. Rake the soil smooth.

PLAN Set up a watering system. Drip is ideal for many plants, but soaker hoses work too.

GROUP SIMILAR PLANTS Avoid mixing plants with differing cultural requirements; if you treat plants with varying needs alike because they're planted together, some will perform poorly.

PROVIDE ROOM TO GROW Allot plants enough space to reach their full sizes. It's tempting to cram them closely together when they are small, but a crowded plant never grows well.

SOAK Water plants still in their nursery containers with a hose before planting.

PLANT Slide the rootball out of the container and gently loosen the roots on the sides with gloved hands. Using a shovel, dig a planting hole roughly twice as wide as the rootball and about as deep. Set the plant in the hole. Trees, shrubs, and perennials should sit about an inch above grade to allow for settling. If your native soil is loam and drains well, backfill the hole with it. If it's sandy or heavy clay, mix compost into the backfill (except when planting natives).

SPREAD MULCH To prevent weeds and help retain moisture, lay 2 to 3 inches of mulch (such as fine bark) over the soil around plants. Avoid piling it against trunks, crowns, or stems, as that can cause rot.

NURTURE NEW GROWERS All young ornamental plants—even natives and drought-tolerant choices—need deep watering right after planting. Irrigate them deeply and thoroughly with the hose, even if you plan to let drip irrigation take over later. Give them regular water through the winter if rains are slight, and then beyond until they reach maturity at a year or two.

CREDITS

PHOTOGRAPHY

Annie's Annuals & Perennials: 274 middle; Caitlin Atkinson: 21 bottom, 24 left, 55 bottom, 99 top, 112–113 top, 167; Debra Lee Baldwin: 121, 146–147, 152, 156 right, 171 top, 173 top, 183 bottom right, 195 second row; Ball Horticultural Company: 267 top left; Marion Brenner: 12 top, 38 bottom, 43 top, 45, 46 bottom, 49, 52 top, 76–77, 114–115, 169 top, 228–229, 242 top, 260, 274 left; Rob D. Brodman: 183 top, 273 top left; Jennifer Cheung: 10 left, 29 top, 35 bottom, 42–43, 55 top, 142 right bottom, 155 bottom, 184–185, 195 bottom #3, 201 bottom, 205; Jennifer Cheung and Steve Nilsson: 221 middle; Stacie Crooks: 78–79, 126; Darcy Daniels: 73 top, 89 bottom right, 94–95 (all), 122 bottom right, 131 left, 132 top left, 132 bottom left, 136–137 (all), 207 bottom, 221 bottom; Terry Donnelly: 6–7 top, 7 bottom, 10 right, 14–15; Tim Fitzharris: 4–5, 10–11 top, 12 bottom, 13 bottom; Paul Furman (baynatives.com): 6 right; Eric Brandon Gomez: 23; Thayer Allyson Gowdy: 50–51; John Granen: 241 bottom left, 267 second row #2, 276–277 bottom; Art Gray: 245 top; Caroline Greyshock: 28–29, 189 left, 217 bottom, 223 bottom; Bret Gum: 160–161 (all), 163 top right, 165, 170–171, 171 bottom, 174–175, 195 third row, Back cover center right; Steven A. Gunther: 18–19, 89 bottom left, 142 bottom #1, 151 top, 151 bottom, 153 bottom, 166–167, 235 top right, Back cover bottom; Audrey Hall: 30–31, 287; Saxon Holt/PhotoBotanic: 8–9, 32–33, 52 bottom, 54–55, 56 left, 57 right, 64–65 top, 88 top right, 88 middle right, 88 bottom left, 91 top, 92–93, 104, 105 top right, 107 top, 110–111, 113 bottom,

117 top, 118 bottom, 120 bottom, 141 bottom right, 142 top right, 145 bottom #4, 158–159, 164 bottom, 168–169, 172, 182, 188, 198 left, 198–199 bottom, 200–201, 226–227, 229 top left, 229 bottom left, 231 bottom left, 232–233, 248–249, 249 top, 249 bottom, 252, 253 top, 253 bottom, 265 bottom, 267 bottom row #3, Back cover center left; D. A. Horchner: 75 bottom left, 99 bottom, 101 middle, 103 bottom, 109, 221 top, 274–275 middle; D. A. Horchner/Design Workshop: 11 bottom, 96 bottom, 100–101, 124–125, 131 right, 134–135 (all), 201 top, 207 middle, 219 bottom, 227 bottom; Joseph Huettl: 214–215; Jon Jensen Photography: 18, 63 top, 105 bottom, 202 top, 258 bottom; Andrea Jones/Garden Exposures Photo Library: 31 top, 276–277 top, 277 top (both); Erin Kunkel: 93 middle, 105 top left, 112 left, 124 bottom, 177, 180, 195 top right, 250–251, 251 top; Scott Lankford: 204–205; Heather Lenkin: 190–191; Holly Lepere: 186, 222, 223 top, 230–231, 281; Chris Leschinsky: 82, 84–85 top, 103 top, 116–117, 156 left, 163 top left, 181, 191 middle, 191 right, 210 top, 210 bottom, 211, 213 top, 224–225, 235 middle right, 247 right, 270 left; David Duncan Livingston: 20–21; Charles Mann (courtesy of highcountrygardens.com): 118–119; Joshua McCullough, Phyto-Photo: 34, 43 middle, 43 bottom, 63 bottom, 66 bottom, 73 bottom, 83 top, 85 bottom, 128–129, 145 second row, 176–177 top, 202 bottom, 217 top, 241 top left, 247 left, 251 bottom, 264, 276 bottom left; Karyn R. Millet: 49 top, 267 top middle; Kimberley Navabpour: 142 bottom #3, 270–271, 271 right top, 271 right bottom; Lauren Springer Ogden: 29 bottom; Jun Ohnuki, Lenkin Design: 242 bottom; Pacific Plug and Liner: 273 middle right; Jerry

Pavia: 44 bottom, 48–49, 89 top right, 93 top, 93 bottom, 96 top, 108 top, 130 right, 149, 159 bottom, 164 top, 178, 195 bottom #2, 209, 235 bottom middle; Victoria Pearson: 46 top, 46–47; David E. Perry: 22–23, 27 top, 68–69, 70 bottom, 72–73, 74–75, 75 top, 80 top, 81, 108 bottom, 111 bottom, 118 top, 122 left, 122 top right, 130 left, 133, 138–139 (all), 163 bottom, 169 bottom, 208–209, 218–219, 235 top left, 274–275 bottom, 288; Linda Lamb Peters: 58–59, 83 bottom right, 141 top #3, 141 bottom left, 142 second row right, 145 third row, 179 right, 189 right, 215 right, 220–221, 229 right, 245 bottom, 267 bottom left, 267 bottom row #2, 271 bottom left, Spine; Norm Plate: 206–207; Trina Roberts/Grin: 80 bottom, 183 bottom left, 262 right; Lisa Romerein: 193, 239, 272–273 bottom; Andrea Gómez Romero: 219 top, 259; Thomas J. Story: Front cover, 1, 16–17, 24–25, 25 bottom, 26–27 (all), 36–37 (all), 86–87, 145 top right, 148, 176 left, 192 right, 203, 212–213, 216, 236–237, 244–245, 254 (all), 256 left, 261 (both), 262 left, 262–263, 265 top, 268–269, 272–273 top, 273 top right, 275 top right, 275 bottom, 278; Terra Nova® Nurseries, Inc. (terranovanurseries.com): 273 bottom right; Steve Terrill: 13 top; Stefan Thuilot: 40–41, 62–63, 77 top; E. Spencer Toy: 142 third row right, 267 top right, 267 third row right, 276 top left; Tish Treherne/Bliss Garden Design: 21 top, 31 bottom, 38 top, 52–53, 56–57, 64 left, 79 top, 84 left, 192 left, 256 right, 258 top, Back cover top; Sarah Warto, Boxleaf Design: 154–155 top, 243; Rachel Weill: 66–67 top, 88 top left, 88 middle left, 141 top #4, 145 top left, 196–197, 207 top, 238, 246, 267 second row #1; Michele Lee Willson: 8 left, 77 bottom, 213 bottom; Michael Woodall:

150–151; Doreen L. Wynja: 6 left, 15, 35 top, 39, 41 top, 41 bottom, 44 top, 60–61, 61 top, 61 bottom, 65 bottom, 67 bottom, 70 top, 71, 75 bottom right, 79 bottom, 83 bottom left, 90, 91 bottom, 97, 98, 101 top, 101 bottom, 102–103, 106, 107 bottom, 117 bottom, 119 top, 120 top, 124 top, 125 right, 127 bottom, 132 right, 141 top #1, 141 top #2, 141 2nd row, 141 3rd row, 142 top left, 142 bottom #2, 145 bottom #1, 145 bottom #2, 145 bottom #3, 153 top, 154 left, 157, 159 top, 162, 173, 179 left, 187 top, 187 bottom, 195 top left, 195 bottom #1, 195 bottom #4, 198–199 top, 210 middle, 227 top, 231 right, 235 middle left, 235 bottom left, 235 bottom right, 240–241, 241 right, 249 middle, 274–275 top, 276 middle, 277 bottom right; Doreen L. Wynja for Monrovia Growers: 111 top; Steve Young: 257

SPECIAL THANKS

We'd like to thank the designers, plant pros, and businesses (listed below), who so generously responded to our many questions.
Annie's Annuals & Perennials, Arterra Landscape Architects, Debra Lee Baldwin, Ball Horticultural Company, Boxleaf Design, Stacie Crooks, Darcy Daniels, Desert Landscape Design, Karen Ford, Ryan Fortini, Paul Furman/ Bay Natives, Margie Grace, John Greenlee, Flora Grubb, Paul Hendershot, Judy Kameon, Kenneth Philp Landscape Architects, Lankford Associates, Lenkin Design, Steve Martino, Daniel Nolan, Pacific Plug and Liner, Chad Robert, Janet Sluis, Joe Stead, Robin Stockwell, Rebecca Sweet, Terra Nova® Nurseries, Stefan Thuilot, Tish Treherne, Molly Wood

OLIVE ALLÉE

Gnarly-trunked olive trees arch over a pair of boxwood (*Buxus microphylla japonica* 'Green Beauty') and purple-flowered Mexican sage (*Salvia leucantha*) in this Montecito, California, garden. Designed to complement the home's Mediterranean style, the garden is both easy care and water-wise.
DESIGN Rob Maday Landscape Architecture

INDEX

Even in a small flower bed, tough but beautiful plants can be stars on the garden stage.

Sunset

©2015 by Time Home Entertainment Inc.
1271 Avenue of the Americas, New York, NY 10020

Sunset is a registered trademark of Sunset Publishing Corporation.

All rights reserved. No part of this book may be
reproduced in any form or by any means without the prior written
permission of the publisher, excepting brief quotations in
connection with reviews written specifically for inclusion in magazines
or newspapers, or limited excerpts strictly for personal use.

ISBN-13: 978-0-376-03012-2
ISBN-10: 0-376-03012-7
Library of Congress Control Number: 2014940101

Printed in the United States of America.
First printing 2015

OXMOOR HOUSE

CREATIVE DIRECTOR Felicity Keane
ART DIRECTOR Christopher Rhoads
EXECUTIVE PHOTO DIRECTOR Iain Bagwell
MANAGING EDITOR Elizabeth Tyler Austin
ASSISTANT MANAGING EDITOR Jeanne de Lathouder

SUNSET PUBLISHING

EDITOR-IN-CHIEF Peggy Northrop
CREATIVE DIRECTOR Maili Holiman
PHOTOGRAPHY DIRECTOR Yvonne Stender

WESTERN GARDEN BOOK OF EASY-CARE PLANTINGS

EDITOR Kathleen N. Brenzel
WRITER Sharon Cohoon
MANAGING EDITOR Judith Dunham
DESIGNER Christy Sheppard Knell
PRODUCTION MANAGER Linda M. Bouchard
PHOTO EDITOR Linda Lamb Peters
IMAGING SPECIALISTS Tom Hood, E. Spencer Toy
PROOFREADER Lesley Bruynesteyn
INDEXER Mary Pelletier-Hunyadi
PROJECT EDITOR Lacie Pinyan
ASSOCIATE PRODUCTION MANAGER Amy Mangus

TIME HOME ENTERTAINMENT INC.

PUBLISHER Margot Schupf
VICE PRESIDENT, FINANCE Vandana Patel
EXECUTIVE DIRECTOR, MARKETING SERVICES Carol Pittard
PUBLISHING DIRECTOR Megan Pearlman
ASSISTANT GENERAL COUNSEL Simone Procas

See page 280 for more acknowledgments.

To order additional publications, call 1-800-765-6400
For more books to enrich your life, visit **oxmoorhouse.com**
Visit *Sunset* online at **sunset.com**
For the most comprehensive selection of *Sunset* books, visit **sunsetbooks.com**
For more exciting home and garden ideas, visit **myhomeideas.com**